# FAMILY CYCLES

How Understanding the Way You Were Raised
Will Make You a Better Parent

## DR. WM. LEE CARTER

NAVPRESS ⬤
BRINGING TRUTH TO LIFE
NavPress Publishing Group
P.O. Box 35001, Colorado Springs, Colorado 80935

The Navigators is an international Christian
organization. Jesus Christ gave His followers
the Great Commission to go and make disciples
(Matthew 28:19). The aim of The Navigators is to
help fulfill that commission by multiplying labor-
ers for Christ in every nation.

NavPress is the publishing ministry of The Navigators. NavPress publications are tools to help
Christians grow. Although publications alone
cannot make disciples or change lives, they can
help believers learn biblical discipleship, and apply
what they learn to their lives and ministries.

Library of Congress Catalog Card Number:
    93-717
ISBN 08910-97481

Some of the anecdotal illustrations in this book
are true to life and are included with the permission of the persons involved. All other illustrations
are composites of real situations, and any resem-
blance to people living or dead is coincidental.

All Scripture quotations in this publication are
taken from the *HOLY BIBLE: NEW INTERNA-
TIONAL VERSION*® (NIV®). Copyright © 1973, 1978,
1984 by International Bible Society. Used by permission
of Zondervan Publishing House. All rights reserved.

Carter, Wm. Lee.
    Family cycles : how understanding the way you
were raised will make you a better parent / by Wm.
Lee Carter.
        p.  cm.
    ISBN 0-89109-748-1
    1. Parenting.   2. Adult children of dysfunctional
families—Psychology.   I.  Title.
HQ755.8.C39   1993
649'.1—dc20                                    93-717
                                               CIP

Printed in the United States of America

FOR A FREE CATALOG OF
NAVPRESS BOOKS & BIBLE STUDIES,
CALL 1-800-366-7788 (USA)
or 1-416-499-4615 (CANADA)

# *Contents*

# *Preface*

In my counseling practice, I am privileged to work with families from all walks of life. One thing I have learned is that we all have more in common than we have differences. One common ground we all walk on is the reliving of our past—we all do it. While none of us can claim a past history with identical details, we all find ourselves reflecting on the impact our early life has had on us today.

One fact developmental psychologists have taught us is that by the age of five years, each of us has established strong personality tendencies. Much of our energy during the remainder of life is spent reacting to the tendencies that were set during those formative years. If that sounds depressing to you, hold on for a moment. The same experts offer good news, as well.

Adulthood brings an ability to understand the past in a way that was not possible during childhood. As we grow older, we each have the capacity to put the pieces of our personal puzzle together so that they make a more complete picture. We are able to make sense out of our past.

This is a book about parenting. Unlike many books on this subject, I will not focus strictly on behavior management strategies or communication techniques, although I hope you will learn a lot about both as you read the following pages. My desire is to help you think through your past so you can answer important questions about your present role as a parent. Questions such as:

- Why do I feel the way I do about myself, my spouse, my parents, my children?
- What habits of communication have I accumulated that I need to reconstruct?

7

- How is my past recycled through the behavior of my children?
- How can I stop a negative cycle?
- What do I do with the emotions that well up within me?
- Is my way of handling emotions good or bad?
- How can I learn to think differently so I can change some habits I have that get in the way of family unity?
- What tools do I need to rebuild failing feelings of self-worth that are a result of my past?

Many hurting parents find themselves living in the past. My desire for each of you is that you learn to live through your past so that your present family life will be all God intended. I strongly believe that no matter how difficult the circumstances of the past, an adult can learn from it and grow as a result of it.

As I reflect on my own past history, I find myself making sense out of the behavior patterns of my own family. It is an enjoyable exercise for me to think through the reasons for the actions and beliefs of my parents and even my grandparents. As I understand their lives, I can understand myself more completely. I then find myself free to pass along my insights about life to my children.

The person for whom I am most appreciative in helping me make sense of who I am is my wife, Julie. Julie and I regularly engage in long conversations about the things we are learning about ourselves in our journey through life. We find ourselves contemplating the effects of our past on our present relationships with each other and our three daughters. These talks pay positive dividends in the way we play out our roles as mother and father.

I look forward to the day I can talk with Emily, Sarah, and Mary about the lessons they have learned from their own childhood as they seek to be all they can be as parents. I am sure I am making mistakes that affect them, but I simultaneously hope that I can be a part of the solution as they make whatever adjustments they feel are needed later in life.

My hope and prayer is that this book will propel you to view your relationship with your children in a way you have not seen before. I hope that in this book you will find bits of God's love that are meant just for you.

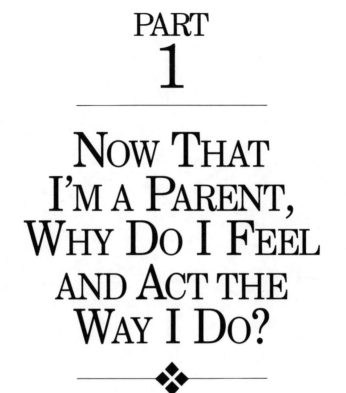

PART

# 1

---

# Now That
# I'm a Parent,
# Why Do I Feel
# and Act the
# Way I Do?

❖

---

CHAPTER

## ❖ 1 ❖

# Can I Break the Chains from My Past?

**"I** feel a need to talk with you about my past." Merle shifted rather uncomfortably in her chair as a signal that she was about to discuss a difficult matter with me. "I had a horrible relationship with my mother. I don't know how you would define an abusive parent, but I feel I was abused by my mother."

I listened carefully as Merle continued: "Most people thought of my mother as a kind, religious woman. In public she said all the right things and gave others the right impressions. At home she was overbearing and constantly critical of me and my sister."

Merle was deep in thought as she recalled her family relationships from the past: "I can hardly remember my mother saying a kind word to me. You can't imagine the arguments we had when I was a teenager. I think their effects on me are permanent. I'll never forget the day my mother told me she hated me and wished I had never been born. Those words still haunt me as a constant reminder that I was unwanted by my own mother."

Merle was having difficulty talking but seemed determined to learn how her past history affected her present behavior. As she paused to regain her composure, I responded, "Even now, it's hard to separate your feelings about yourself from your stormy relationship with your mother."

Merle nodded as she began to sob softly. "As much as I hate the way my mother treated me, I see myself acting in the same way toward my daughter. When I first became a mother, one promise I made to myself and to my child was to be a better parent to her than my mother had been to me."

Knowing Merle was harboring guilt over her broken relationship with her preteen daughter, I responded, "Somehow things have not turned out the way you expected them to."

Merle shook her head with remorse. "No, they haven't. I seem to have no control at all over my emotions. When my daughter does something I disagree with, I lose control of myself. I say things I regret and do things I know are harmful. After my emotions have passed I apologize to my daughter. She usually ignores my apologies. I guess I can't blame her. I never wanted to accept any words of apology from my mother, either."

"The cycle you and your mother were in during your childhood is being repeated with your own daughter. You want to get out of that cycle." Merle looked up at me with a hopeful expression.

"That's what I want more than anything else. I want to break the cycle of emotional abuse that hurt me so badly and now is hurting my daughter."

During her childhood years, Merle knew something was wrong in her family. Though she could not identify in sophisticated terms the dysfunction of her family, the emotional discomfort within her told her something was drastically amiss.

Like most children and teenagers, Merle held on to the hope that her mother would change her parenting style to one that was more considerate and understanding. Whether unwilling or unable to respond with understanding, Merle's mother failed to meet her daughter's emotional needs.

As Merle grew into adulthood and became a mother, she lacked the knowledge and experiences that made a healthy parent-child relationship likely. Having no other reference point to use as her guide, Merle simply responded to her daughter in the same way her mother had reacted to her.

I explained to Merle that there was reason to be encouraged

about her future prospects for building a better relationship with her daughter. Merle's recognition of her own dysfunctional behavior was a first step in the healing process. The support and educational components of the counseling process could equip her with the necessary tools to change the direction of her family life.

As we examine our family histories and the way in which our past affects our current family relationships, three truths about family relations become immediately evident. Comprehension of these truths can mark a starting point for personal growth.

## THE PAST IS PERMANENT, BUT WE CAN LIVE IN THE PRESENT

It is tempting to look back on our past and second-guess what might have been if circumstances had been different. As I talk with people about their family background I frequently hear sentences that begin with "If only . . ." or "I would have . . ." or "I regret. . . ." As we analyze our past, we can readily identify the mistakes others have made at our cost. Circumstances that adversely affected us jump out of our memories.

While it is helpful to understand the harmful effects of our past, dwelling on unchangeable circumstances can be a depressing experience. As I counseled Merle, she learned that she continued to blame her past history for her current family struggles. She recalled that as an adolescent she continually thought, *I would be happy if only my mother treated me with greater respect.* Although she no longer lived under her mother's parental guidance, she still clung to that thought by believing, "I could be a better parent today if only my mother had treated me with more respect as a child."

There is good news for those, like Merle, who feel chained to their past experiences. Adulthood brings a capacity to take charge of the decisions we make as we shape our relationships with others. Merle learned to change her thoughts and eventually was able to state, "I would have been happier as a child if my mother had treated me with more respect. Now that I am an independent adult, I can make my own decisions about how I will choose to relate to others." Each of us has the opportunity to change our interpretation of ourselves. We do not have to be bound to past events.

EFFECTIVE PARENTING SKILLS CAN BE LEARNED

During my childhood and adolescence, computers were not as commonly accessible as they are in today's world. Computers were huge machines used in business and industry that were of no personal value to someone like me.

In the past several years, the computer industry has changed drastically with products now available to even the youngest school-aged child. Though I realized the computer's value several years ago, I was afraid to try my hand at one because I had no training in computer use nor understanding of the multiple uses to me.

Those friends of mine who had a computer continually assured me that I would gain great pleasure from owning one if I would only let go of my fears and learn a new skill. For years I resisted, then finally gave in to peer pressure and bought a computer. With a little study and instruction from others with more experience, I am now fairly proficient at using my personal computer. I have even been known to make statements such as, "I don't know how I ever got along without my computer."

In the same way that I was afraid to acquire new skills on a computer, many of us are afraid to acquire the new skills needed to build satisfying relationships with our children. Though the past may be an uncomfortable memory, we tend to cling to it simply because it is known territory.

Each of us can learn skills to enhance our relationships with those we love most. Breaking cycles of hurt involves opening ourselves to new understanding and better ways of getting along with others.

In working with Merle as she sought to rebuild the damaged relationship with her daughter, we focused on building a new understanding of the emotions God had given her. We talked of the way she defended herself against potential emotional harm. We looked at how continual growth in her emotional and spiritual completeness could benefit her as a mother. Through this new understanding she was able to improve her effectiveness as a parent.

Each of us enters adulthood with habits acquired during childhood and adolescence. Some of these habits are good, while others need to be discarded and replaced with new skills. Merle found that it was her habit to immediately try to force her opinion on her daughter when they disagreed. Habit had taught her to yell and scream to solicit cooperation from a stubborn child. New skills emphasizing listening to her daughter replaced her tendency to assume that she knew her daughter's needs. Consistently following through with promised consequences supplanted the threats she previously made.

Merle and I shared a common fear. We both were afraid to step into previously unknown worlds. I learned through experience that a computer would not bite me. It could be a valuable tool for my personal needs. Merle learned that parenting is an art form that can be fine tuned with careful learning experiences. Each of us can become students, learning skills that draw us closer to personal wholeness.

## ❖ GIVING UP CONTROL OVER OTHERS ❖

As Merle and I talked, the term *control* surfaced with regularity. She spoke of how her mother controlled her. She mentioned feeling out of control as a teenager, and said she now felt out of control as a mother. She told me she wanted to bring her daughter under greater control.

The desire to force control in our relationships almost always results in failure. In a predictable way, as we try to exert control over others, the intensity of the relationship grows. Continual effort to control relationships only heightens tension in those relationships. Our well-meaning efforts increase the potential for interpersonal harm.

In human relationships, it is true that we have control only over ourselves and no one else. As a part of God's design, each of us was made with the capacity to make choices about the way we interpret ourselves and our relationships to others.

As I counseled Merle, she learned that dwelling on the shortcomings of her past history was of no value. She had no control over her past. She also determined to refrain from making choices for her daughter. She had no control over her daughter's desires.

Merle realized, however, that she had complete control over a variety of personal matters. It was her choice to interpret her past independent of the present. She could reject her own mother's disregard for her personal worth. She could choose to disagree with the parenting tactics her mother used. She could disregard the negative comments her mother made toward her and substitute more positive beliefs in their place.

Merle learned that she had control over her reactions. She could set limits by which her daughter could choose to abide. Merle could select her reaction to her daughter based on her daughter's display of judgment. She also recognized that she could choose to remain calm when her daughter tried to draw her into an argument. By making these and other choices, Merle influenced her daughter, but refrained from trying vainly to control her.

My aim throughout this book is to identify those skills needed to break cycles of defeat in family relationships. I have found that understanding our most dominant emotions provides a useful beginning to personal change. We will look at harmful ways we, as parents, protect ourselves against emotional pain in our reactions to our children. Symptoms the child may display as a result of our emotions and defensive postures will be examined. Direction will then be offered as we seek to make the personal changes that can result in both personal satisfaction and family fulfillment.

❖ 2 ❖

# Why Can't I Control My Emotions?

**M**r. Anderson was exasperated that his son, Darian, was disobeying yet another rule. The boy had been told countless times not to run in the house. As the young runner zipped down the hallway, his dad caught him by the arm. The look on his dad's face was frightening to the eight-year-old.

"Darian, this is the last time I intend to tell you not to run in this house!" He squeezed the boy's arm tightly and shook him. "I guess you don't know how to walk. I'll make you hurt so bad you can't run!" With that said, Mr. Anderson whipped his son soundly on the backs of his legs.

"Dad, I'm sorry! I didn't mean to run. I promise I won't do it again!" Darian had been punished by his father many times before. He hated the vindictive way his dad tried to enforce limits in the home. He was fearful of his dad's temper, knowing his dad was capable of losing control of his emotions.

"Saying you're sorry just isn't good enough!" Mr. Anderson continued to spank the boy. Darian thought his dad would never let go of his arm.

"Dad, that hurts! Stop!"

Mr. Anderson momentarily stopped the spanking and put his face in the face of his son. "Why should I stop punishing you? You don't seem to understand the rules around here, so I'm going to make sure this whipping makes you think a little harder the next time you feel like running in the house!" With those words Mr. Anderson spanked his son one more time.

Finally free from his father's grasp, Darian cried as he hurried to his bedroom to be alone. As he walked away, he mumbled, "I hate you."

"What did you say?" Mr. Anderson had heard his son's muttering and dared the boy to repeat his expression of scorn.

Screaming, Darian repeated his statement: "I said 'I hate you'!" He then bolted to his room and slammed the door behind him. A furious father followed him and gave him an even more forceful dose of punishment.

Darian's father wanted to restrain the boy's impulse to run in the house. Through punishment, his intent was to teach the child respect for a reasonable rule of household conduct. Yet, in reaction to Darian's rule violation, Mr. Anderson lost the reins on his own impulses and showed the young person a frightening display of emotion. He rationalized his behavior through his assumption that Darian needed a strong show of force to learn respect for his authority.

Rather than show respect for his father's position of family leadership, Darian reacted to his father's explosion with a strong statement of contempt for all that his father stood for. The authority this father had forced on his son provoked the negative emotion of hatred. Not to be emotionally strangled by an eight-year-old, the dad angrily whipped the child further after his authority had been rejected. The father who had hoped to teach his child control of his impulses displayed no control over his own.

Mr. Anderson related this incident to me as he described the behavior problems of his son. As I got to know this man further, I recognized in his emotional makeup scars from a past that was void of healthy family relationships. Mr. Anderson explained that the whippings he gave Darian did not compare to the childhood beatings he had received from his own father.

As this man told of his past, he recounted many lessons he

gleaned from his father's treatment of him. Even though he hated his father's calloused ways, he had deduced that force was the only way to teach a child responsibility.

Lack of control over emotional impulses is a frequent cause for family discord. Feeling an emotion, the adult may express it without regard for the impact of his behavior on the impressionable child. The impulsive parent has several identifiable emotional qualities that stem from his past history.

## IMPERFECTION IS DIFFICULT TO TOLERATE

As the past histories of adults with limited control over their impulses are examined, we often find a family history of intolerance. The adult may have been sent frequent communications as a child that imperfection was unacceptable. Adults may have received this message from their parents in these ways:

- Forceful expressions of opinions ("It's right because I say it's right!")
- Use of emotional intimidation ("If you don't do what I say I'll. . . .")
- Show of strength through physical force ("No child is going to overpower me!")
- Demonstrated emotional toughness ("If I show tenderness, my child will think she can manipulate me.")
- Few expressions of approval ("I don't need to reward my child for doing what he is supposed to do.")
- Frequent expressions of disapproval ("If I don't tell my child what she did wrong she'll never change.")
- Use of corporal punishment ("I'll teach that child a lesson he will never forget!")

Many impulsive adults, like Mr. Anderson, come from family backgrounds in which tolerance for individual needs was not expressed. The emphasis in the home was on the child's mistakes and not on his successes. Without being taught as a child that mistakes form opportunities for learning and improvement, he entered adulthood with the mistaken belief that errors are not acceptable. Rather than view the child's errors as opportunities for positive intervention, the impulsive parent reacts quickly, and often angrily, to the inevitable mistakes of the child.

A cyclical pattern is encouraged through impulsive parental behavior. As the adult quickly attempts to stamp out the child's mistakes, he creates an array of negative reactions in the child. Feeling personally invaded on an emotional level, the child often strikes back to defend himself. Seeing the child's defensive posture as evidence of a need for more force, the parent reacts impulsively once again as the cycle goes unchecked.

The impulsive parent is often known to say, "If I could only get my child to think about what he is doing, he wouldn't make so many mistakes. Then I wouldn't have to punish him so often." Ironically this parent reacts to his child's mistakes with an intolerance that prevents him from displaying the forethought he expects in his child. As children are prone to do, the young person gives greater attention to the behavior of the parent than the words spoken by the adult. The experience of the child is a study in intolerance of others' mistakes.

## LACK OF FAITH IN OTHERS

A parent who was raised in a home where trust was not displayed learns to mistrust his own children. *Trust* is a word we often misunderstand. Applied to family relationships, trust is shown when the parent believes his child can appropriately respond to his guidance. The trusting parent has faith that the child will learn of his substantial potential as he progresses through the stages of life.

Mr. Anderson told me of the lack of trust he had been shown by his parents, especially his father. Although he recognized that his parents' reactions to him were a model of mistrust, he had been thoroughly convinced that unless a child is blasted into submission he will inevitably fail in life.

In one of our sessions Mr. Anderson told me, "I just assumed my father knew what he was doing when he exploded and whipped me. I knew I didn't want him to punish me constantly, so I always did what he told me to do."

"Even though you tried to do what your father expected, you couldn't do everything according to his wishes," I responded. "Otherwise, you wouldn't have memories of your father being so harsh."

I assumed that even though Mr. Anderson said he followed his father's strict rules, he did not feel affirmed by his father's negative reactions.

"Oh, I never did anything right, according to my father! Nothing was good enough for him. I remember feeling that I was a failure in his eyes."

I asked Mr. Anderson to draw from his childhood experiences the beliefs he had come to embrace about the level of trust he should show others, especially a child. His response was interesting. "Maybe my father didn't think he could trust me, but I didn't lose faith in myself. Deep in my heart, I knew the way my father thought of me was wrong. I think I trust other people, even children, in spite of my father's mistrust."

Wanting Mr. Anderson to think from his child's point of view, I asked him if his son Darian would agree that he was a trusting father. "I don't see why not. What have I done to show him I don't trust him?"

I remained silent as Mr. Anderson and I reflected on his statement. With a slight smile this man questioned me, "You think I'm wrong, don't you?" I smiled. I did not need to elaborate on what he had just concluded.

When a parent reacts impulsively to a child the message is sent, "I must act quickly to erase your mistake. I must stop you from making errors because you are an incapable person." The strength of this message is underlined by the intensity of the parent's emotion.

## PLACING BLAME ON OTHERS

One way adults keep the focus off their own impulsive behaviors is to lay blame on the child for the problems that arise in family life. Mr. Anderson was known to tell Darian, "If you didn't act the way you do, I wouldn't have to punish you." Impulsive people generally fail to consider the full impact of their own outbursts on the child's subsequent actions. Because a knee-jerk reaction is given to a child's mistakes, he has limited opportunities to learn more appropriate ways to meet reasonable adult standards. The guilt that overwhelms the child pushes him to continue in his inappropriate behavior. The blame he receives for being a disruptive force in the family only confirms his belief in his inadequacy.

### ❖ REPLACING IMPULSIVENESS WITH PATIENCE ❖

Many of the books in the New Testament are letters written to various groups of Christians. The first letter Paul the apostle wrote to the people in Thessalonica closes with words of guidance for those in leadership roles. He tells his readers that leaders are in a position deserving honor and respect. He gives his sanction to their efforts to guide others spiritually. Paul further advises leaders to "help the weak, be patient with everyone. Make sure that nobody pays back wrong for wrong, but always try to be kind to each other."[1]

The parent assumes the leadership position of the family and is certainly deserving of respect and honor from his child. Accompanying that respect, though, is the instruction that the leader act in ways that invite others to follow his direction.

Impulsive parents lack the training that comes through childhood interactions with family members who teach the skills of tolerance and patience. Encouragement is more than just a way of talking positively to a child. The encouraging parent knows that by example he can teach the child restraint over his urges.

In Darian's relationship to his impulsive father, his disrespect for his father was a sign of revolt. He was revolting over the rigid control his father tried to enforce in the household. Though his behavior needed redirection, his desire for the affirmation of a trusting father was valid.

CHAPTER

## ❖ 3 ❖

# *Why Do I Feel So Isolated and Alone?*

"**M**y daughter is my best friend," Anna told me as we discussed her family relationships. "In fact, she's the only close friend I have." While I was pleased that Anna felt so close to her seventeen-year-old daughter, I was concerned that her child was not just her best friend but her only friend.

Anna continued, "If it weren't for Sandy, I don't know where I would be in life. I've never really believed anyone else loved me. You can't imagine how alone I've felt all my life. I have to keep Sandy close to me. If I lost her, I'm afraid to think of what I would do to myself."

Anna was in her early forties. She described her childhood and adolescence as being uneventful. "That's part of my problem," explained Anna. "Nothing really bad has ever happened to me, but nothing good has happened to me, either." Her early years were bland and void of the kind of family assurances that would convince her she had a place of importance in her world.

Anna rarely had argued with her parents or siblings as she grew up. She was considered a responsible person. Her father worked long hours for a railroad and was frequently gone overnight. Her mother was a nurse with an irregular work schedule. Anna recalled spending many nights with her two older brothers while her parents worked. As a child she seldom played with other neighborhood children. During her teenage years she was socially inactive.

Anna married George at nineteen, although she realized later that she married more for the convenience of a relationship than out of love and commitment. Marriage was a desperate chance to experience the closeness she'd never received from her own family. Her hopes were dashed during her first years of marriage when she received little more affection from her husband than she had from her parents.

Anna gave birth to two children. A son was born four years before Sandy. Feeling unsure of how to relate to her son, Anna became emotionally dependent on Sandy for the affection she so desperately sought. The two were inseparable during Sandy's childhood. In many ways, Anna relived her own fantasies of childhood bliss through her daughter.

Anna and George eventually divorced after sixteen unhappy years. When their son finished high school he left home, seldom making contact with his mother and sister. Anna became completely absorbed in her relationship to Sandy, more than ever before. In our counseling sessions Anna continually told me, "I just don't know what I'll do when Sandy leaves home. I can't bear the thought of losing her and being all alone again."

Over the next few years Anna did all she could to keep her daughter emotionally tied to her. She bought Sandy whatever she could afford and made it financially attractive for the teenager to stay at home once she turned eighteen and went to work. The mother and daughter duo did virtually everything together.

During one session, Anna revealed how gripping her loneliness was. She stated, "Sandy has gained almost fifty pounds since she turned eighteen. I have to admit, I'm kind of glad she has. She hates the way she looks and doesn't want to go out with other people. You may tell me I'm wrong to think this, but as long as she feels that way about herself, I know I can keep her with me."

Anna's feelings of loneliness ran so deep, she invested in her daughter's unhappiness so she would not venture away from home.

Loneliness causes an adult to feel empty and separated from others. Lonely people, like Anna, often feel desperate. At the root of this emotion is the frustration of being misunderstood. Lonely people typically want relationships very badly. At the same time, they fear relationships because experience has failed to give them the confidence that they can succeed interpersonally.

## COMMUNICATION SKILLS MAY BE DEFICIENT

An unfortunate byproduct of loneliness is the lack of opportunity for meaningful communication with others. Childhood and adolescent experiences have taught the lonely adult to keep his feelings to himself. Anna failed to develop communication skills largely because her parents were inaccessible to her. Her lack of social experiences kept her from learning to interact with her peers. Rather than learn how to groom relationships, she maintained a safe distance from others.

Consider the following family dynamics that could also contribute to loneliness in a person:

- As a child, Terry was quiet and unassertive. His aggressive father did not understand the boy's unassuming ways. He frequently encouraged his son not to be a "baby" but to assert himself like a man. His father's dominance over him encouraged Terry to crawl into a shell of isolation.

- Dorothy recalled spending most of her childhood and adolescence chasing the elusive goal of popularity. Her family life centered around the quest for social status and prestige. Even though Dorothy experienced what others would consider significant social successes, she was never satisfied. For every honor she achieved, her parents pushed her toward another.

- For years Reggie had been known as a "clown." He was always good for a laugh in a group. By himself, however, Reggie suffered feelings of depression that few people knew about. Growing up in a home with alcoholic parents convinced him he had to work hard to be noticed. Though he enjoyed being in the public eye, the attention did not quench his desire for real family togetherness.

In each of these scenarios an adult emerged from childhood unable to express his needs for affection and belonging in an honest way. Childhood feelings of misunderstanding can push a person to disguised communication. Failed communication attempts result in unrelenting feelings of rejection and alienation.

## SENSITIVITY TO OTHERS MAY BE UNBALANCED

People who are lonely are often the nicest people to be around. Keenly aware of the discomfort that accompanies social isolation, they frequently go out of their way to accommodate the needs of others. In fact, a lonely adult may be so accommodating he neglects his own needs in favor of others.

My counseling sessions with Anna taught me that she was most sensitive to her daughter's needs. When Sandy was young, Anna was completely absorbed in meeting her needs for affection. By providing for Sandy's physical and emotional care, Anna experienced a closeness she had never felt toward anyone else. She enjoyed their relationship so much she found herself unable to separate her own needs for friendship from Sandy's.

When Sandy was a child, her mother was her constant companion and playmate. Anna told me she thought she and Sandy were simply very close, when in reality the two were so dependent on one another for emotional satisfaction their two lives had become one.

As Sandy grew older, her friends saw her as socially inept and avoided meaningful contact with her. As a preteen, Sandy clung more tightly to her mother, who reciprocated with behaviors that kept the mother and daughter tightly bound to one another.

Anna's sensitivity to her daughter's needs for affection were out of balance. By investing herself in Sandy's life, Anna hoped to satisfy some of her own unmet needs for approval. While this mother cherished her relationship with her daughter, she unwittingly promoted in Sandy the same feelings of isolation that plagued her.

INTERPERSONAL RELATIONSHIPS ARE VIEWED WITH FEAR
As we study human relationships, we realize the irony in many of the behaviors we display. It is not uncommon for a lonely adult to state he wants relationships with others, while simultaneously fearing the prospect of personal closeness to another person.

Fear typically accompanies loneliness. This fear may have its roots in a number of past family circumstances. A lonely adult's fear may be a result of any of the following:

- Repeated failures in attempts to assert feelings to others.
- Lack of opportunity to learn the skills needed to interact successfully.
- Mistrust of others, resulting from personal traumas such as abuse or neglect.
- Doubt of self that has been generated by criticism from family members.
- Disappointment, following deception at the hands of significant persons in the past.
- Frequent disapproval from family members coupled with limited affirmation.
- Enduring humiliation or emotional pain as a result of being repeatedly taken advantage of by others.

Through the experience of fear, a person learns to avoid those circumstances or people who cause feelings of discomfort. Many emotionally balanced people recall confronting fear and driving it out of their system of emotional control. However, others have experienced fear that is enduring, causing them to feel unable to overcome it.

## ❖ BREAKING OUT OF ISOLATION ❖

In John's gospel we are given a rather lengthy account of an encounter Jesus Christ had with a lonely woman.[1] We have come to refer to this woman only as "the woman at the well." This woman's emotional isolation from others was evident in a variety of ways. She came to draw water from the well at a time when she knew she would not be confronted by others. Apparently her reputation was such that she was poorly regarded.

Through her conversation with Christ, we learn that she had been in and out of failed relationships with men. When asked by Jesus about her current marital status, she attempted to deceive Him. Her life was such a shambles, she did not want others to know her hurt.

Despite her loneliness, the woman at the well recognized in Christ the opportunity to revive a lost sense of self-worth. The lack of judgmental spirit in Christ's response alerted her that the new life He promised was genuine and attainable. Accepting His assurance that He was the Messiah, the prophesied Savior, she immediately took steps to free herself from the pains of loneliness that had characterized her life to that point.

We must assume that the conversation this woman had with Christ created in her a realization that her value as a person went beyond the successes and failures she experienced with others. Recognizing that she had an eternal worth to God that could not be stripped from her, she opened herself to the kind of relationship that would introduce meaning to her troubled life. Accepting the nonjudgmental character of Jesus as evidence of the eternal love that could be hers, she immediately began to reframe her concept of herself.

The woman's reaction immediately following her conversation with Christ is interesting. She left her belongings at the well site and ran back to her town to bring others to meet and understand the Messiah she had just come to know. We can only imagine the townspeople's astonishment as she approached them with assertive behavior. I would suspect that she normally related to others in the silent and often distressed way that characterized her loneliness.

As this woman discovered, loneliness is dispelled when two things occur. The first is the recognition of the sense of importance that is a trait of all of God's creation. Understanding the eternal value attached by God to men and women can replace lonely feelings with a sense of purpose and meaning.

Second, this woman refused to wait passively for others to set aside their prejudices about her personal character. She assertively approached them with a message about the change she had made in herself as a result of her unusual encounter with Someone who looked deep within her soul. Among other things, her behavior sent out the message, "I'm a new person! I no longer view myself as an isolated person who has no place in this world. I want others to enter into the world of meaning I have found."

Like the woman at the well, each of us has the opportunity to view ourselves as worthy in relation to Christ. Additionally, we each have choices that are ours regarding how we will relate to others. Instead of waiting for others to change their views of us, we can assert ourselves with the belief that our knowledge of our own eternal value gives us something valuable to share with those around us.

# ❖ 4 ❖

# *Why Do I Worry So Much?*

"**C**arol, I'm scared." Nine-year-old Kristine curled up next to her older sister as closely as she could. It had become her habit to sleep in her sister's bed as many nights as Carol would allow it.

"What's wrong this time?" Twelve-year-old Carol did not want to tell her obviously distressed sister to go back to her own bed, but she was tired and needed to rest.

"I heard Momma fighting with Daddy again. I'm scared that something's going to happen to Daddy."

"What could possibly happen to Daddy? Momma can't do anything to him." Even though outwardly Carol seemed unconcerned about Kristine's anxiety, inwardly she was fully aware of the reason for the younger girl's worry. When Momma got mad at Daddy, she was unrelenting in her verbal abuse of him.

"Carol, I just don't want tomorrow to be bad. That's all I'm worried about. If Momma keeps talking to Daddy like that, you know what she's going to be like in the morning. I'm scared they're going to keep fighting and won't quit."

Carol was now as concerned as Kristine. She held tightly to her sister's sweaty hand and tried to comfort her: "It's going to be okay, Kristine. Just stay in here with me tonight. Maybe it won't be as bad in the morning as you think." The two girls lay quietly as they continued to hear the awful sounds of arguing in another part of the house. A scared and worried Kristine hardly slept that night. She dreaded the coming of the next morning. Even though her mother's wrath was shown to her father, the girl knew she would suffer from the pain of her parents' conflictive relationship.

❖     ❖     ❖

As the now grown Kristine told me stories about her past, she cried. She hated to relive those days, which had been marked by one conflict after another between her parents. She identified her mother as the catalyst for most of the arguments that took place in the home. She was forever picking on her downtrodden husband for the inept way he bumbled through life.

Kristine wanted to make sense of how her family's dynamics affected her current family relationships. She saw many of the same harmful qualities of both parents in herself and wanted to get out of the cycle of defeat that surrounded her marriage and parent-child relationships.

Kristine and I spent time building a framework around the personalities of each of her parents. Doing so allowed her to comprehend the origin of her anxious tendencies toward her own family members.

Kristine described her mother as emotionally cool and aloof. She was weak in her ability to communicate through words. She chose, instead, to telegraph her feelings to others nonverbally. If she felt slighted, she simply refused to speak to the person who offended her—sometimes for days at a time. If she wanted to be left alone, she withdrew into her bedroom without explanation. When she wanted to dominate, she gave her children a glare that dared them to cross her. She rarely spanked or even scolded her children. As Kristine explained it, "My mother didn't have to scold me. I knew from the way she talked to Daddy that I didn't want her to talk to me like that. When she gave me a certain look, I knew I had better do what she expected."

Kristine recognized many symptoms of depression in her mother. She was prone to awful mood swings and was impossible to please when in a foul mood. More than once she threatened to kill herself following a fight with her husband. Once after such a statement, she left the house for several hours, leaving Kristine petrified that she had followed through with her threat.

Kristine spoke with both affection and disgust when describing her father. He was one of the kindest men she had ever known. He would go out of his way to give a hand to someone in need. Never one to meet a stranger, he commonly made friends with whoever would spend a minute talking with him.

Despite his congenial nature, Kristine's father was almost completely irresponsible. He rarely got anywhere on time. If he said he would do something, he could not be depended on to get around to it anytime soon. Though he loved his children dearly, they knew not to count on him for family leadership. He was too passive to be in a position requiring that he assert himself. It seemed that this man limped through a beleaguered life. Though Kristine hated to admit it, her father had many inadequacies.

## ACCEPTING THE PROBLEMS OF OTHERS AS YOUR OWN

The kind of family dysfunction experienced by a child like Kristine can take its toll in the form of chronic worry and anxiety during adulthood. Family life marked by marital conflict, broken communication, limited parental control, and constant fear leaves a lasting imprint of anxiety on a child.

Kristine entered adulthood early. She recounted that by the time she reached high school, she had already peaked in her maturity. She was not interested in the normal adolescent activities of her peers. In her mind, life had too many more serious problems to warrant activities that had no value other than to entertain or occupy time. Though not wanting to look down her nose at her friends, she felt more responsible than the average teenager.

As a child Kristine learned to take responsibility for the emotional tempo of the home. When her mother was in one of her awful moods, the child pretended not to notice. She did all she could to cheer her two siblings, and even her father. Despite her efforts, the entire family knew there was a damaging emotional void. It felt better, somehow, to ignore it.

When Kristine saw a family member engaged in an activity sure to raise the ire of her mother, she quickly stepped in to intervene. Though her siblings or father may not have understood her mission, she felt it her duty to do what she could to keep peace in the family. She even scolded her father for his irresponsible ways, telling him he could avoid many arguments simply by doing what he was supposed to do.

Anxiety has a way of gripping an adult who has waded through family wars. Worry can warp the adult's sense of responsibility. Bothered by the constant effects of early conflict, the adult, like Kristine, may be duped into the belief that it is preferable to take charge of potential problem situations so they can be immediately squelched. To allow potential conflict to be carried out is seen as too risky a move. In the eyes of the adult from a dysfunctional family, any conflict is bad. It almost certainly results in emotional pain.

## COMMUNICATION IS SUPERFICIAL

Worry is accompanied by a fear that if the grim realities of life are confronted, they may actually come true. Pessimism convinces the worrier that it is better to avoid life's difficulties than search for solutions.

In the communication of an adult who has endured a childhood full of dysfunctional relationships, the following characteristics may be found:

- Difficult circumstances are portrayed as not as bad as they seem to be.
- Obvious flaws in relationships are shrugged off or even ignored.
- Listening to the feelings of others is a painfully difficult task.
- Solutions are forced on problems whether or not they are appropriate.
- Communication is waged on a nonverbal level rather than openly.
- Realistic solutions are dismissed as unworkable.
- Negative feelings are often channeled through physical complaints.
- Dialogues may quickly turn into arguments.

- ◆ Negative feelings are not allowed proper expression.
- ◆ Feelings get hurt easily because of a tendency to misinterpret others' intentions.
- ◆ Telltale signs of family distress are overlooked.

When Kristine married, she thought she had found a companion she could trust to bring her out of the chaos that had dominated her family of origin. During the days she and her husband dated prior to their marriage, she felt she could relate to him honestly. After they were married she found it almost impossible to feel close to her husband. She loved him, but could not express it by being affectionate or by trusting him with her inner thoughts.

As Kristine and her husband had children, she knew they would bring her personal satisfaction. Yet, as her children grew, she found a rift forming between herself and the children whose love she cherished most. She was unable to separate the fears that dominated her own childhood from her worry about relatively insignificant family matters.

Kristine told me, "I know my children and husband think I'm a nuisance. I worry all the time about what could go wrong at home. They think I'm nagging them. That's not my intent. My intent is to keep my family from experiencing what I went through as a child."

Kristine communicated her fears to her family in a disguised manner. Feeling she could single-handedly solve any family problems, she kept family dialogue from being productive. In her own fearful way she broadcast the message, "If you have a problem, we don't need to discuss it. Just give it to me. I'll take care of everything." While the design of this form of communication was to prevent family dysfunction from reoccurring, its actual effect was damaging.

## ALL EMOTIONS EXCEPT ANXIETY ARE SUPPRESSED

When anxiety is present, all other emotions are given a back seat. One faulty belief that accompanies anxiety is that if the floodgate of feelings is ever opened, the deluge will never cease. The result is an accumulation of emotional baggage too heavy to carry. The child of a dysfunctional family learns to be numb to those gnawing feelings inside that suggest discomfort. But, no matter how numb a person might be to his emotions, they still impact his sense of personal satisfaction.

Notice the way the person who has accumulated emotional baggage may inappropriately suppress his emotions:

- Angry feelings are dismissed as invalid because anger is not allowed.
- Guilt is interpreted as a deserved consequence for mistakes that have been made.
- Loneliness is accepted as an inevitable way of life.
- Phoniness is displayed as an alternative to the real feelings hidden within.
- Blame is absorbed for the faults others display.
- Obvious discomfort is ignored through denial.
- Shame is felt over the mistakes others make rather than put in its proper place.

To return to Kristine's case, she built a family communication system as an adult that disallowed negative feelings from being discussed. She felt that if her husband and children could be forced to look on the bright side of life, there would be few of the relationship problems that plagued her childhood. As Kristine and I talked, she realized that this deliberate suppression of her emotions created an emptiness within her. The family discord she wanted to avoid went underground. Though her family was not outwardly argumentative, problems were never solved because it had become her rule to disallow negative emotional expression.

### ❖ REORDERING YOUR PAST ❖

The anxiety that accompanies a person into adult life is aimed at controlling the fears of earlier years. Once a more relaxed state is achieved by the adult she can begin to reorder the events of her life. Placing the past dysfunction of a family into its proper position releases the adult from the stranglehold of worry and anxiety.

As Kristine and I began to dissect her past, she came to several realizations:

- Her family's argumentative ways were not of her choosing. She did not contribute to her parents' decision to live in a disharmonious way.

- Her mother's depression was a byproduct of her own interpretation of her life's circumstances.
- Her father's inadequacies represented a feeble effort to shield himself from the discomfort he experienced daily.
- Her current anxiety represented fear over her childhood. It was no longer useful to her.
- She could not control the way anyone else in her family felt or behaved. Her past efforts to do so failed. Her current attempts to control her husband and children also had failed.
- Her worth as a person was independent of the emotions and behaviors others displayed toward her. Her value did not depend on how others felt or acted.
- Disagreement with family members does not equal or indicate a loss of love for them. Neither does emotional detachment from the dysfunctional ways of a family equate a lack of love.

As an adult, each of us has the capacity to look back on the past and interpret it in a way that was not possible during childhood and adolescence. Too often, though, the emotional habits of childhood persist and cause the dysfunction of earlier years to be recycled.

Kristine was able to recognize that the anxiety of her childhood was a reaction to a mother's condemning ways and a father's inadequacy. Her immature mind convinced her during those years that she could control her world through worry. Adulthood brought with it the ability to see the fallacy of her early thinking. She found that a new direction in life was possible.

CHAPTER

## ❖ 5 ❖

# *Why Am I Sad*
# *When I Want to Be Happy?*

When Sherryl was a teenager her mother was relieved
that somehow her daughter had made it through many
trying circumstances. In this mother's eyes, Sherryl
had endured constant family turmoil without noticeable signs of
emotional harm. Sherryl was an only child who had been forced to
grow up in a hurry because of her mother's poor judgment in choosing
marriage partners.

Sherryl seemed unbothered by the fact that her mother had been
married three times. Each marriage was as bad as the previous one.
Her mother, Patsy, had a "bleeding heart" and tended to be attracted
to men who needed her care. Two of the men Patsy married were
alcoholic. One of these men also battered her physically. Her third
husband seemed different at the outset of their marriage. He did
not drink and was more emotionally subdued than her previous
husbands.

Despite his gentle nature, he was frequently unfaithful to Patsy.
What started out as a congenial relationship ended like the two previous marriages, in a nasty split. The only thing that kept Patsy
going was the fact that her daughter progressed easily through

childhood and adolescence, creating no additional problems.

Not until Sherryl entered adulthood did problems surface. She lived what she called a "split lifestyle." One side of her personality was responsive to others and conscious of her responsibilities. This aspect of her character caused her to be successful in college and later in her career. Those who knew this side of Sherryl spoke in glowing terms of her positive nature and her ability to get the job done.

Sherryl had a darker side that few people knew about. In her early twenties she increasingly became consumed with her outward appearance and eating habits to the point of developing bulimia, an eating disorder. On her lunch hour at work and later when she was at home, she would consume large quantities of food. Feeling bloated, she would purge her body of all food and then exercise excessively. Her husband thought she was simply a fitness nut. In fact, he was rather proud that his wife wanted to stay in shape. He didn't become aware of her problem until two years into their marriage.

Sherryl knew her emotions and behavior were unhealthy. Over the course of her first ten years of motherhood she wove in and out of her eating-disordered behavior pattern. At times she thought things were going well for her and that she had a grip on her past difficulties. At other times she felt overwhelmed with impulses she could not control and spent weeks and even months living out her secret life of emotional and physical self-destruction.

Sherryl's behavior suggested a complex web of emotions. Though her mother had been pleased that as a child Sherryl seemed so resilient to the many traumas in their family, these events had taken a heavy toll on her emotional stability. As I got to know Sherryl, it was clearly evident that she was experiencing depression. Sherryl knew that this emotion was within her, although she had difficulty explaining it.

THE PAST CAN PROVOKE GUILT

As Sherryl began to uncover the family dynamics of her past, she understood the guilt and anger associated with her dissatisfaction. Throughout her childhood and adolescence she had been a source of strength for her mother. In many ways Sherryl had been given the reins of leadership in her home as a child. While her mother was involved in unsatisfactory relationships with men, the mother-daughter relationship gave Patsy her emotional breath of life.

In adulthood, Sherryl felt the inevitable repercussions of her childhood experiences. No longer able to contain her own emotions and dissatisfaction over her past history, she began to react emotionally and physically. Not a verbally expressive woman, she channeled her painful emotions through an eating disorder.

The emotion of guilt emerges in adulthood when inappropriate reactions have been given to past circumstances. Sherryl was never allowed the opportunity to express her emotions of anger and dissatisfaction at the instability of her family. When she was young she felt she simply had to maintain a positive outlook on life because her mother depended so much on her for emotional stability.

Expressing emotions openly is natural and normal for a child. After all, no child likes the constant upheaval that results from chronic conflict and discord within a family. Yet, instead of expressing this anger, Sherryl withheld her feelings, hoping they would go away. She seemed to be successful in her emotional development until adulthood placed its own set of responsibilities on her. Then she collapsed.

Sherryl told me that she felt responsible for her mother's happiness. As she talked about her relationship with her mother, she seemed to be pronouncing herself guilty for crimes she could not possibly have committed. She felt as though she had been a stumbling block to her mother's marital satisfaction. Somehow she had become convinced that unless she was perfect, her mother's life would be even more unhappy than it already was.

## CHILDHOOD LOSS CAN CREATE ANGER

Creating anger within Sherryl was the fact that she had no relationship with her father. She was bitter that he was alcoholic and had neglected his family obligations. She regretted that she hardly knew him. At one point Sherryl told me, "I have a friend whose father died several years ago. As this friend told me about the loss she felt at her father's death, I could identify with her. Even though my father is still living, I feel as if he died when I was a child."

Sherryl had difficulty thinking of herself as one consumed with anger. She could hardly openly acknowledge that she disliked her past life. Instead, she acted out this emotion by giving her body a physical and emotional beating through her eating habits. She was internally punishing herself for her parents' failure to provide for her emotional needs.

When we think of the emotion of grief, we often tend to think of it as a reaction to a loss resulting from the death of a loved one. Yet, feelings of grief can be aroused by other losses as well. In many cases an adult finds that she has failed to grieve the loss of a family relationship because there has been no closure to that loss. As in Sherryl's case, the effect of the breakup of a family unit may be lost in the fact that some contact is maintained with each family member. The consequence may be a delay in the necessary grief process needed for healing to take place. Putting off these emotional expressions until adulthood may result in unresolved emotional pain.

## DENIAL OF REALITY PREVENTS HEALING

A feeling of shock typically accompanies a sudden loss. The intent of this God-given emotional reaction is to allow the person time to make adjustments to the loss. Yet, prolonged denial of the reality of a loss prevents the healing process from progressing through its natural course.

Ways in which a person may engage in denial include the following:

- Blaming uncontrollable circumstances for harmful events.
- Offering excuses for the behavioral choices of others.
- Reacting negatively to those who offer help.
- Blaming oneself for the actions of others.
- Refusing to consider alternative points of view.
- Holding on to the belief that things will soon return to normal.
- Refusing to talk about painful emotions.
- Pretending that circumstances are not as bad as they seem.

I believe God gave each of us all of our emotional capabilities with the intent to benefit us in some way. The initial reaction of shock to a family loss helps the young person buy the time needed to regain emotional composure. The short-term denial of reality can be a useful coping tool. However, prolonged denial resulting in a refusal to accept the facts of life creates a myriad of harmful internal reactions.

Often adults find themselves burdened with unresolved feelings because of the lack of past parental leadership in guiding them through their pain. With nowhere else to go but inward with their emotions, they enter adulthood carrying unnecessary childhood grief.

## ANGER TAKES ITS TOLL

Many emotional reactions are present in the feeling of anger. Not only can we be mad about situations beyond our control, we can also feel frustrated, hopeless, bitter, or confused. As we examine the harmful circumstances of early life, we often find that we do not understand the feelings that raged within us.

Sherryl was very young when her mother divorced her father. She did not know why her mom and dad could not get along. She knew only that family relations were strained and emotions were out of control. Unable at the time to comprehend her feelings and having no outlet for expression, she simply held them within. As she grew older and more aware of the bitterness she felt toward her past, she continued to stuff her feelings deep within rather than assert her emotions. She was afraid of the unhappiness she would bring to her mother if she openly acknowledged her anger.

I encourage adults who have difficulty with angry feelings from their past to step away from their adult world of thought for a moment and enter again the world of their childhood. As adults correctly see and understand their angry emotions from the past, they can begin to bring closure to the traumas that are preventing happiness in adulthood.

As Sherryl and I worked together to understand her angry feelings, she was able to acknowledge more fully the loss of control that had gripped her life. She viewed her eating habits as an odd way of regaining some sense of control over her emotions. Her perfectionistic tendencies were loosened as she realized that she could be happier when she let go of her need to hold tightly to her anger.

## PREOCCUPIED WITH SADNESS

When pleasant family experiences have been forfeited because of past conflicts, it is normal to feel sad about the trauma of that loss. Every child has a way of naively hoping to breeze through a perfect childhood. As adults, we are too often painfully reminded that perfect families are hard to find. We learn to adjust our expectations of family life to be more realistic.

Childhood optimism keeps many young people hoping that the elusive dream of the perfect family will be realized. While an optimistic outlook can be a saving grace to a child, it can also be a hindrance to honest emotional expression.

Masking sad feelings beneath the hope of family reconciliation that may never occur allows depressed feelings to set in. As adulthood arrives, thoughts of depression may dominate behavioral choices. Thoughts that often accompany this condition are expressed here:

- I was cheated out of the childhood I deserved.
- I don't know what it's like to feel the security of a close family.
- People don't really understand what I've been through.
- If I had had a happier home life, I could have accomplished more with my life.
- I feel as though my family held me back from doing the things I wanted to do.
- My shame kept me from building the friendships I could have experienced.
- My family's unhappiness gives me an empty feeling.
- I wonder what my life would have been like if things had been different.
- I wish my parents could have experienced a greater joy in their life.

Letting go of sadness is difficult at best. Sherryl told me, "The hardest thing for me to grasp as I look back on my past is that no matter how noble my thoughts are, there's not a thing I can do to change the past. I just feel helpless." I find that saddened and grieving adults need a sense of hope and comfort for the future. We all need something positive to believe in, even if that hope is that the past will provide lessons that will prevent its reoccurrence.

I asked Sherryl to spend several days thinking about the following questions:

- What were you protecting yourself from when, as a child, you behaved in such a perfect manner? What are you protecting yourself from now by your compulsive behaviors?
- Do you need to protect yourself from your family's disharmony now in the same way you needed protection as a child?
- What feelings, such as anger, did you withhold as a child? Were those valid feelings? Are you still withholding emotions?
- In what ways do your past family circumstances still dictate to you how you will act and feel today? How does this affect your current relationship with your spouse? With your children?
- How can you redirect your desire for happy family relationships into positive activities? Are there any restraints holding you back?

As Sherryl let go of feelings of sadness, she felt unburdened of the need to bring alive a family unity that could never be realized. In place of her depression, she found an optimism that strengthened her. Recognizing that her defense against emotional harm from her family was no longer needed, she let it go and replaced it with the positive view that she should give to her husband and children the very sense of security she had lacked as a child.

### ❖ LOOK FORWARD RATHER THAN BACKWARD ❖

Perhaps more than any other obstacle to personal growth, we hold on to feelings of grief about days gone by. We can become prisoners to events over which we had no control. Furthermore, there is absolutely no chance of changing the past.

Sherryl realized she was allowing her past to dictate her present and future satisfaction. Not only did it spell defeat for her, it caused her to experience guilt that she was creating bad memories for her own children as well. She did not want to allow the cycle of personal discontent to continue another generation.

❖       ❖       ❖

King David stated in the psalms, "Though I walk in the midst of trouble, you preserve my life; . . . with your right hand you save me. The LORD will fulfill his purpose for me; your love, O LORD, endures forever."[1] These words, contained in a psalm of praise, offer hope for a person troubled about the past. David briefly mentioned the reality of "trouble" in his life, but quickly shifted his focus to the future. Rather than assume that the past was destined to be relived, he anticipated with confidence that his future would be one of fulfillment.

Through our counseling sessions, Sherryl learned that she looked to the future with a certain sense of dread. Her fear was based on the assumption that she could not overcome the harmful effects of a past that had not met all her needs. She learned, as the psalmist had, that fulfillment in life can come regardless of the events of the past. God has a plan for the future that has our best interests at heart.

Fulfillment is achieved when we understand that we are being prepared by our God for successful living in the future. Past events need not dominate our present or future. God has for each of His creations a desire for wholeness. Our responsibility to God, with His help, is to set aside long-held feelings of grief, denial, anger, guilt, and depression. As we allow our emotions to teach us about the present and prepare us for the future, we can move forward with the assurance that personal fulfillment can become a reality.

# ❖ 6 ❖

# *Why Am I So Self-Centered?*

S even-year-old Jeffrey handed a note to his mother. The little boy did not know the exact contents of the note, but he knew he was the bearer of bad news. Jeffrey's mother, Jane, took the note and opened it. It was from her son's teacher at school. The note explained how Jeffrey had gotten into yet another fight on the school playground. The words seemed all too familiar to Jane. She could only shake her head in disgust as she read of her son's poor behavior.

After Jane finished reading the note, she sighed heavily. She was tired of having to discipline her son for his frequent errors. "Go on outside," she told Jeffrey. "We'll decide what to do about this when Dad gets home." Jeffrey was glad he did not have to face immediate judgment, but he was not looking forward to his dad's arrival later that evening.

When James walked into the house that evening, Jane gave him the silent treatment. Bothered by his wife's obvious anger, James demanded an explanation. Exploding, Jane said, "I'll tell you what's wrong with me! Jeffrey came home today with a note from his teacher, telling how he got into another fight at school. I'm mad because he's just like you were! I'm afraid he's headed for some rough days unless things change pretty soon."

James and Jane had had this conversation before. James knew exactly what Jane was implying with her words. His wife feared their son would go through a stormy childhood and adolescence just as he had endured years earlier. James felt both defensive and guilty. He did not want to be given responsibility for his son's behavior, yet he knew that Jeffrey had learned many actions from him.

Wanting to stop their son's destructive pattern of behavior before it got out of hand, James and Jane made an appointment at my office. During our first session, James told me, "I want you to be bluntly honest with me. I know I have not lived what you would call the perfect lifestyle. I did a lot things wrong when I was young. Jane is probably right when she says I have a lot to learn about how to handle children. All I know is that I was unhappy when I was young, even though I wouldn't admit it to anyone at the time. I don't want to see Jeffrey go through the same things."

GROWING UP SPOILED

Time allowed me to learn details of James' past. He grew up in what he described as a normal family. Both parents worked and provided James and his brother all they needed to meet their physical and social needs. In fact, James told me, "If anything, my parents gave me too much. Life was easy for me when I was young. I didn't think I had to follow the rules. Rules were for other kids. I always ignored what others told me to do."

Both of James' parents were passive adults. They were unassertive with their children, giving them considerable leeway in deciding how they would act and with whom they would associate. "I was a spoiled little brat," James told me. "I'm thirty-two years old, and I'm just now learning that the rules others have to follow apply to me, too."

James reconstructed many of his past behaviors for me. As a child he lost his temper quite easily. He was quickly annoyed when others told him what to do. "Even if they were right, I insisted that I knew what was best for me. I was so hard to get along with it was easier for my parents to just give in rather than fight with me."

The lack of regard James had for rules extended into the school setting as well. Having been taught that he was the exception to the rule, James was haughty around adults. He ignored their attempts to solicit his cooperation. As a teenager he joined his older brother in a wide range of deviant behaviors. He seldom came home when he was told to be home. He did pretty much as he pleased. Scrapes with the law were not uncommon. In fact, as a teen he saw arguments with police officers as evidence of his manhood.

Laughing, James explained to me, "Hey, we were just being boys." I knew, as did James, that the rule violations of his youth went beyond normal teenage mischief.

"I used to believe that week days were a time to rest up for a hard and wild weekend. From about the time I was fifteen until after I got married, I partied and drank beer all weekend long. I guess you could say I was an alcoholic. I know that's what everyone else said about me."

❖　　　❖　　　❖

Adolescence is a time when many individuals "sow their wild oats" in an attempt to find their true identity. While adults often look back on the blatant errors of days gone by and simply shake their heads in disbelief, the effects of past errors can linger into adulthood.

## RELATIONSHIPS ARE NOT A ONE-WAY STREET

A lifestyle marked by carefree, impulsive behavioral choices virtually requires a lot of attention. A self-centered approach to gratifying needs is common for a person who has adopted this lifestyle. For people like James who have been raised with few demands and responsibilities, giving to others is difficult because it is not an acquired skill. Self-centered teenagers can enter adulthood willing to receive all they can from others, but reluctant to give in return.

Relationships, then, are mistakenly viewed as a one-way street. The immature adult is insensitive to others' needs. Bothered by the conflict that often surrounds relationships, he cannot understand why others would fail to cater to his whims. Beliefs this adult may bring into his family relationships include:

- My desires are met first, then yours will be considered.
- I'm not interested in the things that bother others.

- Someone else can take responsibility for mistakes that
  are made.
- I'll let others take care of the unimportant details of
  family life.
- I don't want others to come to me with their emotions.
- If I have extra time, I'll spend time with the family.
- I don't feel the need to discuss my feelings with others.
- Others should do as I say and not as I do.

Most adults do not carry on with the same misbehaviors that marked their earlier years. Yet, while adults may not engage as freely in rule violations, they are often deficient in relationship skills.

James told me in his own blunt fashion, "I remember thinking that Jane was my wife, so that meant she was supposed to do whatever I wanted her to do. If I wanted her to ignore my mistakes, that's what she should do. If I gave a weak excuse for my irresponsibility, she was supposed to believe me. I felt that I didn't have to be accountable to anyone."

Not only was James unaccountable to others, he also failed to be accountable to himself. He had no need for commitments. Relationships were viewed for their self-serving value. He was going nowhere in life. His lack of commitment to others doomed him to failing to reach his own potential as a responsible adult.

## EMOTIONS ARE SUPPRESSED

The misconduct of earlier years can put a strain on relationships, taking an emphasis away from honest emotional expression. As James told me, "When I was younger, about the only thing my parents talked to me about was my misbehavior. They always threatened me with punishment. They spent most of their conversations with me trying to convince me to change. I never listened to them."

As I counsel families, it becomes quickly evident to my clients that I place a high degree of importance on the value of family relationships in guiding a child's behavior. Without a healthy relationship between a parent and child, the child is more prone to compete with family members than to cooperate.

The child who is prone to misconduct takes charge, like James did, of the family. He forces his parents to pay attention to his behavior, but wants them to ignore his emotional needs. To the misguided youth, emotions represent an undesired signal that internal change is needed. Unwilling to change to a lifestyle that is more responsive to others, feelings are suppressed.

Because James said he wanted my direct comments, I confronted him during one of our sessions. He was ignoring Jane's plea that he simply listen so he could understand the emotions she felt. James chuckled when I bluntly pointed out that he was running from an emotion-laden issue. "You got me on that one," he admitted. "I hate to say it, but I don't know what to say when Jane, or anyone else, wants me to talk about how I feel about something."

Though it was a painful experience for him, James spent the next few minutes simply listening to Jane. When she had finished talking, I asked James to identify emotions that his wife had just expressed. It was a difficult experience, not because James lacked intelligence, but because he was unskilled in recognizing the emotions of others. His past experiences had taught him that emotions were to be ignored. His task in adulthood was to learn to trust his emotional instincts so he could more easily relate to others.

## FRUSTRATION TOLERANCE IS LOW

The adult who has lived a hard life since childhood finds it difficult to tolerate the stress that inevitably enters adult family life. Having been accustomed to a lifestyle that is self-centered, it is hard to share the spotlight with others. James explained to me that the birth of their first child was perhaps one of the most difficult experiences of his life.

"I thought it would be just great having a baby son. I had told Jane that having a child would probably help me grow up. I know she was hoping it would help me be a more mature adult! I still can't believe how jealous I was of the baby. I wanted Jane to do everything for me, but she couldn't. She had the baby to take care of instead of me."

"It was quite an adjustment for you to take a back seat to an infant. I suspect you didn't tolerate your child's demanding lifestyle." I wanted to know more of what James had learned during those early days of parenthood.

"To tell you the truth, I didn't know what I was going to do. I didn't want to leave Jane and the baby, but I sure didn't enjoy having to jump just because the baby cried and Jane said she needed my help."

Low frustration tolerance is a byproduct of the self-centeredness and inability to respond to others' emotional needs that results from whirlwind youthful experiences. This lack of tolerance can be expressed in these ways:

- Irritability in the presence of normal family crises.
- Demanding that others keep their needs to themselves.
- Speaking to others with an aggression that attempts to be overpowering.
- Refusing to look at matters from alternative points of view.
- Throwing temper tantrums as a poor expression of dissatisfaction.
- Refusal to listen to others' points of view.
- Distorting the facts to meet personal desires.

It is a difficult lesson for many adults to learn, but as we are more accepting of the needs of others, our satisfaction in relationships increases.

James told me, "Once I finally realized that Jane and the kids had a right to their feelings, I lost some of the intensity of my own emotions." James nonverbally kicked and screamed as life taught him that he was hurting himself by his intolerant attitude. He was surprised at the relatively easy pace found in a lifestyle that took into account others' needs in addition to his own.

### ❖ BECOMING AN ADULT ❖

I have previously related the story of James and his change from a "wild and crazy" young person to an adult with a deep compassion and concern for his family and others. People have asked how a person as unyielding and self-centered as James could make the kind of adjustments he did in his adult life.

❖          ❖          ❖

In the Bible in the book of Acts, we are given the details of a change that took place in the life of perhaps the Bible's most famous character, except for Jesus Christ Himself. Paul the apostle changed from a rebellious and aggressive young person who was calloused to others to one who could later in life counsel, "Let your gentleness be evident to others."

The historical character of Paul and the modern personality of James both had personal qualities that were rechanneled from a negative expression to one that was more positive. Youth often is accompanied by confusion that causes the young person to thrust himself forcefully on others. In the process of his behavioral rebellion, the young person is able to learn of his own frailties, if he is open to the lessons that accompany life's mistakes.

Paul was forcefully confronted with the need to set aside his desire to confront others aggressively with a rigid set of religious practices. James saw the potential for failure in family relationships if he did not learn to respond more empathetically. Both men replaced mistaken points of view with thoughts that were more considerate of others. Yet, both retained the zeal that had driven them in their earlier years.

Before life-changing events take place, it is necessary to confront that internal unrest that signals a lifestyle that is out of control. When Paul was struck by his encounter with God, we can only imagine the sea of thoughts that ran through his mind for days. His change required an entirely new perspective on life. No longer convinced that his self-centered views could be trusted, he learned to accept guidance from those who drew him closer to a dependence on God.

In a similar way, James struggled to let go of his earlier ways of thinking. "It's hard for me to set aside my own point of view and see life the way others do. That's not the way I'm used to thinking," James told me. I explained to James that the beginnings of change actually had their roots in his childhood years. Though he ignored his emotions at the time, he had at least an inkling of discomfort that told him his behavior pattern would eventually lead to relationship damage.

The experiences of life, whether they are as dramatic as Paul's or gradual like James', teach the value of relationships that look beyond personal desires. Listening to the voice of God, whether it booms its message to us or speaks in the form of an emotional tug at the heart, is the beginning of satisfying changes in relationships.

# ❖ 7 ❖

# *Why Do I Feel*
# *So Lousy About Me?*

Susan and Diane had been friends for years. They made a point to get together at least once a month for lunch. During one lunch Susan told Diane about problems she was having at home with her middle child: "I just don't know what to do with Larry anymore. I know I'm not a very good mother." Susan looked to her friend for understanding.

"Who said you weren't a good mother?" Diane confronted Susan in a loving way.

"I don't know. It doesn't take much intelligence to see that I'm not doing the greatest job of parenting. My husband stays mad at me most of the time because of the fights Larry and I get into. I don't need someone else to convince me that I'm not the greatest mother in the world. I'm afraid the evidence against me is pretty strong."

"Susan," countered her concerned friend, "if you don't stop thinking like that you're never going to be the parent you're capable of being. You're not giving yourself credit for your strengths."

Susan wanted to believe what Diane said. As she listened to Diane, she shook her head and muttered, "I don't know, Diane. I've felt this way about myself for a long time. Sometimes I wonder just how capable I really am."

Susan suffered from chronic feelings of low self-esteem. She was convinced that she was not competent to meet the demanding role of the mother of three children. She did her best to fulfill her parental obligations, but was never satisfied with her efforts. She was plagued by the nagging feeling that she was doing something wrong. She loved her children dearly, but worried about the effect of her parenting on their eventual emotional growth.

❖     ❖     ❖

Susan grew up as the youngest daughter of a businessman who was highly regarded in the community. She recalled feeling left out of her father's life as a child. He provided everything for his family—except his love and attention. Susan confessed, "I would have gladly given up some of the finer things in life if only my dad had spent more quality time with his family. Unfortunately, his work came first and his family second.

"I remember when I was a girl I said something to my dad about his lack of attention to me. He seemed to understand at the time. He promised things would get better once his business schedule slowed down. I really don't know if his business required that much from him, or if he simply didn't know how to be a family man. I do know that I felt betrayed when I realized my dad had no intention of living up to his word to me. You can imagine what I felt about where I fit in his life." Susan recalled her family relationships with a sense of frustration.

"My mother bore the brunt of the responsibility for raising the family. When I was young I had mixed feelings about her, too. Of course I loved her, but we had some terrible fights. At the time I thought I couldn't wait to be out on my own. I vowed that if I married and had my own family, I would provide a different kind of life for my children." Susan chuckled at the irony of her words.

"Now I find myself providing the same type of home for my children that I experienced. I really don't have the faintest clue about why I do and say the things I do. I just do things the way my mother did." Susan felt defeated in her attempt to provide the respect for her children she felt she missed as a child.

Perhaps the most important element a parent can bring into family relationships is a healthy image of herself. The confidence of a parent guides her as decisions are made that affect the family. A lack of parental confidence can spell trouble for a family through the loss of effective leadership.

As Susan and I dissected her family of origin we learned that her mother and father both suffered a loss of confidence in their family leadership skills. Her father felt incompetent to involve himself in intimate relationships. He chose instead to focus his energies on business relationships. He felt he was more likely to succeed at the office than in the home. His absence left his wife with the responsibility of caring for the children's emotional needs. In his shortsighted way of thinking, any failure in the family was his wife's concern since family relationships were her obligation.

Susan's mother was overwhelmed with the need to organize a household. She lacked the confidence that her best laid plans would work effectively. To ensure that her children did not stray from appropriate behavior, she became overly invested in their lives. What Susan's mother meant to be parental concern was interpreted by her children as overprotectiveness. The harder she tried to make the best decisions for her family, the more likely she was to experience rejection.

Susan emerged from adolescence with a confused feeling about her personal competence. Her father's lack of attention to her emotional needs taught her she was not worthy of parental affection. Her mother's overbearing manner sent an additional message that she was incapable of making independent decisions. As an adult Susan remained unsure of her worth as a wife and parent. She showed her lack of personal confidence in an awkward approach to family relationships.

## RELATIONSHIP SKILLS ARE POORLY DEVELOPED

With the uncertainty that defines people with low self-esteem comes an inability to relate effectively to others in the family. I find that many adults know how to get along beautifully with those outside their family, but lack the confidence that allows for success within the confines of their own home.

Susan told me, "When I'm with a friend like Diane, I feel no pressure to act according to a prescribed role. I'm free simply to be myself. When I'm with my husband or children, though, I see so many expectations of me in my roles as 'wife' or 'mother' that I simply feel unable to fulfill them successfully."

It is normal for a parent to feel a certain degree of pressure to perform in building family relationships. After all, others tend to base opinions of an adult on the behavior of the entire family. A person, like Susan, who is lacking in confidence will allow the pressures of parenthood to interfere with the development of family relationships that are built on mutual trust and respect.

Weak parental self-esteem can be seen in family relationships in these ways:

- Becoming overly intrusive with family members for fear that they will make insurmountable mistakes.
- Assuming that family members will challenge every decision you make about family matters.
- Becoming easily defensive when the children or spouse question a judgment call you have made.
- Displaying inconsistency in following through with plans because of the fear of failure.
- Second-guessing decisions you have made, especially on issues that have no clear answer.
- Interpreting the differing opinions of family members as a personal rejection.
- Avoiding action on touchy subjects to escape potential confrontation.
- Allowing family members to change your mind easily because their argument seems stronger than yours.
- Frequent emotional outbursts, sending the signal to your family that you can be manipulated.

Self-image problems make relationships within the home difficult to groom effectively. The doubting parent is often afraid to dive to the depths that family relationships require. Underlying that self-doubt in the parent is a fear that to delve too deeply into complex family dynamics may expose personal weaknesses. Though because of this the adult often remains dissatisfied, many uncertain parents maintain a course of unsatisfying relationships simply because it is familiar territory.

## FEELINGS ARE NOT PROPERLY ASSERTED

Most adults with a bruised self-image have strong feelings about themselves. Many will quickly reveal their feelings about themselves to others once they feel comfortable in a relationship. Until trust is built, it is interesting to observe the verbal hedging of people struggling with their feelings of personal worth. Many will do anything but talk about themselves in an attempt to keep the focus off their insecurities.

When I first met Susan, I found her to be hesitant to tell me of her personal concerns. She had come to my office hoping to be filled with the kind of care that would make her lack of confidence disappear. When she realized that my job was simply to help her in her own reconstruction efforts, she felt an initial sense of panic.

After I had gotten to know Susan better, I found her to be virtually unable to stop talking about her feelings about herself. Realizing that she would change in her family relationships only as she changed her view of herself, she became motivated to look at the hidden thoughts that influenced her behavior.

Susan's initial unassertive behavior is common in those who fear change. That fear is a shield from the pain looming around the corner that must be squarely confronted.

These are ways an adult may be unassertive in the presence of others:

- Accepting the opinions of others without questioning their accuracy.
- Keeping feelings within, even though it hurts to feel so misunderstood.
- Viewing others' opinions as superior to those you hold.
- Assuming that others are not interested in what you have to say.
- Feeling guilty whenever negative emotions are experienced and therefore dismissing them.
- Procrastinating until the "right time" presents itself before asserting feelings.

♦ Always allowing others to put their needs first for fear of offending them.

When feelings are held inside without proper expression, they build up to the point that emotional harm results. A weak self-esteem will convince a parent that it is wrong to speak openly about thoughts that may conflict with another's point of view. In an interesting twist of events, a low self-image sets the parent up for mistreatment by other family members.

Finally able to voice negative emotions she had bottled up for years, Susan told me, "You know, I'm really getting tired of the way my husband so frequently belittles me for the way I handle the kids. I also feel I deserve more respect as a family leader from my children. I don't like being the family doormat."

Susan recognized that her self-esteem had previously prevented her from standing up for her own needs for approval and appreciation. As her self-esteem grew stronger, so did her willingness to assert herself in a healthy fashion. Not only did she feel greater inner peace, her family respected her for her stronger leadership.

## MASKS HIDE TRUE FEELINGS

Related to the tendency to be unassertive with feelings, a weakened self-esteem can encourage the parent to assume roles she thinks others want her to play. While it is normal to gauge our behavior to match the social circumstances in which we find ourselves, wearing emotional masks prevents others from knowing our true identity.

Exasperated at herself for her unwillingness to allow others to genuinely know her, Susan told me, "I'm totally disgusted with myself sometimes. When I'm with my friends from church I feel I need to act 'spiritual' even though I know I'm being a hypocrite. When I'm with other friends I know strictly on a social basis, I feel the need to appear 'trendy.' But, when I'm with my children, I need to be 'the perfect mom.' I act out so many roles, I feel confused about who I really am. I know one thing is certain: I'm usually pretending to be someone I'm not."

Self-esteem problems convince us that to be ourselves is undesirable. We can become convinced that to allow others to see what we are really like will open us to rejection. The paradox is that by continually hiding behind emotional masks, we are dooming ourselves to the shallow relationships we wish to avoid. As we develop a sense of comfort with ourselves, we often find that others are not as condemning as we feared they would be. In fact, genuine emotions and behaviors can bring about the relationship satisfaction we so strongly desire.

## ❖ RECONSIDERING YOUR WORTH ❖

A child is like a sponge, absorbing the messages sent by others. Yet, a child does not know how to evaluate those messages. The repeated responses given by parents and others who play an important role in the child's development form the basis of a child's self-concept. Unfortunately, a negative self-image can result from family responses that failed to meet personal needs.

In Susan's case, she assumed that her father's lack of parental involvement indicated that she was not an important part of his world. Her mother's well-meaning, but emotionally charged, way of relating gave her the feeling that she could not make independent, responsible choices. Years of interactions that highlighted Susan's weaknesses and overlooked her strengths convinced her that she was an inadequate person.

The good news that accompanies adulthood is that all of us have the capacity to evaluate our childhood interactions in a way that we were unable to do as children. As adults we have the choice of examining the beliefs that make up our self-concept to determine which personal convictions are useful and which are not.

Susan learned that many of the opinions she held about her own worth were based too strongly on the negative experiences of her childhood. Though she initially had a difficult time rejecting her habitually negative views of herself, she learned instead to focus on her positive qualities and rebuild a crumbling self-concept.

❖          ❖          ❖

King David found himself struggling with his own inadequacies. In prayer, he implored God, "Search me, O God, and know my heart; test me and know my anxious thoughts. See if there is any offensive way in me, and lead me in the way everlasting."[1] David wanted spiritual guidance as he sought to know his strengths so he could put them in the place of his perceived weaknesses. He recognized that he had made faulty judgments in the past. Realizing that the presence of God's guiding hand gave him the chance to reconstruct his personal views of himself, he set about to change his character within the warmth of God's direction.

# PART
# 2

# WAYS THE PARENT PROTECTS HIMSELF FROM THE PAIN OF THE PAST

❖

"Why do you always talk to me this way? You treat me as if I'm a nobody! Don't you know that I have feelings, too? I just want you to understand me!" Eleven-year-old Alicia unloaded her feelings toward her mother. Mother and daughter had just gone around and around about Alicia's irresponsible behavior. Though she had not meant for Alicia to feel like a "nobody," Mother realized she had been too harsh in her reaction to Alicia.

As Mother contemplated her relationship with Alicia, she could not help wondering what she could do to influence her daughter more positively. She worried about the choices her daughter was making and did not want to see Alicia suffer from her own lack of judgment. Mother was frustrated at the way she was unable to express her concern in a way Alicia could understand.

❖      ❖      ❖

Being a parent is a stressful job. Not only does the parent have to contend with the pressures of adult life, in many ways the pressures surrounding the child fall on the parent, too. Interaction between parent and child can serve to teach the child how to handle his own emotions and behavior in a responsible way.

The characteristic way a parent reacts to the normal traumas of daily life is shaped largely by past events. As we have seen, the events of the past influence our view of ourselves and the behaviors we display. Each of us has experienced varying degrees of stress throughout our years of life. We should have learned to handle that stress so it does not become debilitating. Some of the reactions a parent uses to fend off uncomfortable feelings are useful, while others are counterproductive.

It is natural to want to defend ourselves from harm in family relationships. Emotional defenses can act as a prevention against the internal pain that makes life difficult. Yet, rigid defenses against pain are usually a sign that the parent is struggling with his own difficulties, making him unable to expend the kind of energy that makes a family function efficiently.

We may respond to the daily trials of life in two ways. The first is to have an open approach to our relationships that allows for honest communication. The second is more harmful and often involves unconscious ways of defending ourselves against personal fears and anxieties. Greater awareness of these often-unconscious methods of defending ourselves opens us to building relationship skills that increase our effectiveness in family life.

# ❖ 8 ❖

# *Understanding Why*
# *I Can't Stand Conflict*

M r. and Mrs. Walters were called to the school to confer with their son's teacher. "I'm not quite sure how to tell you what Reggie has been doing," stated the teacher as she searched for the appropriate words. "There have been several incidents recently in which things have come up missing. All the evidence seems to point to Reggie."

"You mean, you think Reggie has been stealing?" Mr. Walters asked.

"Well, it does appear that he has. I have to say I haven't caught him red-handed, but I strongly suspect he's been into the other students' belongings. It seems that he is always around when another child reports that they have lost an item. He also has been seen with possessions I know are not his. When I have confronted him with my suspicions, he says that he doesn't know what I am talking about; but I think he may be deceiving me."

Mr. and Mrs. Walters were concerned that their son could be involved in an undesirable behavior pattern. After further discussion, they thanked Reggie's teacher and promised to look into the matter.

Later that evening, the parents sat down with Reggie and told him of their conversation with his teacher: "We met with Mrs. Fields today. She said she is concerned that you may be taking things that don't belong to you. We want you to know that we're not mad at you, but we also want you to know that that kind of behavior cannot be tolerated. It has to stop."

Reggie looked at his parents with disbelief. "I don't know what you're talking about. I haven't stolen anything at school. I would never do that. Mrs. Fields must have gotten me confused with someone else." Reggie seemed sincere in his statement to his parents.

Reggie's dad took the lead in talking to their son. "Let me give you an example of what Mrs. Fields told us. She said that one day last week she noticed you bought an ice cream bar in the school cafeteria. She knew that you normally don't buy ice cream. Another boy said someone had taken money from his desk earlier that day. She suspected you because you sit near him. Can you see why Mom and I are concerned? We agree with Mrs. Fields that you could have been guilty."

Reggie began to cry. "But I didn't take his money! I took my own money to school that day. I just didn't say anything to you about it because I thought you might not let me buy any ice cream. I promise I didn't steal!"

The conversation went on for several minutes with no confession from Reggie. He maintained his innocence and had an answer for every question his parents raised. Satisfied that they had put their son through enough interrogation, they let him go to his room. After Reggie was gone, Mom and Dad talked about their parental dilemma.

"What do you think, Howard?" Mrs. Walters asked her husband.

"I don't think Reggie has done anything wrong." Mr. Walters sounded convinced.

"What makes you so sure Mrs. Fields isn't right?"

"I know Reggie well enough to know when he's lying and when he's telling the truth. Couldn't you see the look in his eyes? That was not the look of a boy who was guilty. Also, I was trying to recall the day Reggie supposedly stole that other boy's money. I'm pretty sure I remember hearing change rattling in Reggie's pants pocket that morning before he left for school. I think he's telling the truth when he says he took his own money without our knowledge. Let's give him the benefit of the doubt. I don't want to punish him when we really don't know that he's guilty."

Mrs. Walters trusted her husband's judgment. They agreed to drop the issue of Reggie's potential deceit and apologized to their son for falsely accusing him.

❖     ❖     ❖

I got to know Reggie two years after this incident took place. He came to see me because he had been suspended from fifth grade for repeatedly fighting and intimidating other children. Reggie told me about his parents' earlier conference with Mrs. Fields. He revealed that he had been "getting away with murder" for quite some time. He knew that whenever he was accused of wrongdoing, he could offer his parents a simple explanation and they would believe him. They would find some way to rationalize his actions. He was seldom held accountable, even when strong evidence suggested his guilt.

I learned a great deal about the Walters' family dynamics by listening to Reggie. He realized that his parents were afraid to be angry with him because they did not want to bruise his emotions by being forceful. Their preference was to believe that their child was incapable of deceit. Mr. and Mrs. Walters had become highly subjective in their thinking and refrained from viewing their son's deviant behavior pattern objectively.

Even though Reggie was now obviously involved in harmful actions, his parents still sought simple explanations for his misconduct. Mrs. Walters told me in Reggie's presence, "I know Reggie did wrong to fight with a boy at school, but I can't really blame him for what he did. I sincerely believe the other boy provoked him. I can't be upset with my son for defending himself."

As his mother made this statement, I glanced at Reggie. His face had an angelic appearance. The look in his eye said to me, "Do you see what I mean, Dr. Carter? My parents will find a way to rationalize anything I do that is wrong."

## IRRATIONAL RATIONALIZATION

When parents rationalize the inappropriate behavior of a child, they are actually being anything but rational. Rationalizing is trying to make an irrational act appear to be rational. Facts are interpreted in a way that allows the parents to feel comfortable. Rationalization, then, is a method of disarming feelings of emotional conflict.

I talked with Mr. and Mrs. Walters about the harm that results from rationalizing and dismissing a child's poor behavioral choices. They were able to see that their son had been taking advantage of them. As we discussed this family dynamic, they offered several reasons why they had been willing to defend themselves against their feelings of anger at Reggie's behavior. Many of these reasons were a result of their own childhood experiences.

- They did not want Reggie to feel as if they did not love him. Both parents had been raised in very strict homes in which little affection was shown. They believed that to deal harshly with their child would send the undesired message that he was not loved. That had been the message they received from their overbearing parents.

- By giving Reggie the benefit of the doubt, Mr. and Mrs. Walters assumed that their son would be appreciative of their trust in his ability to make responsible choices independent of pressure from them. Neither parent had been allowed to think independently during childhood. They were told without reservation what they should think and how they would behave. They did not want their child to feel as they did.

- These parents had learned to be mistrustful of people who got angry easily. In reaction to negative experiences from their own childhood, they preferred to keep their angry feelings to themselves. They believed that only cruel parents get upset with their children. They felt that by dismissing their negative emotions, Reggie would respond by making wise choices.

- Armed with the belief that Reggie was a good child, his parents chose to believe that he would not willfully be disobedient. They interpreted his actions as normal childhood mistakes. They convinced themselves that by being patient,

Reggie would eventually see his error. They feared that he would feel personally condemned if they questioned him for errors they could not prove he intentionally committed.

As Reggie's behavior became progressively worse, the Walters rationalized that to confront Reggie for his misbehavior would only add fuel to the fire. They determined to let time heal their son. Their own childhood experiences had convinced them that family conflict should be avoided at all cost.

The lessons Mr. and Mrs. Walters had learned from their respective childhood experiences had given them a false view of how to function in family relationships. They had been taught by their parents that they were "bad" children through frequent mistreatment when they made mistakes. As they entered adulthood, they set out to correct the errors that had been made by their parents.

During one session, Mr. Walters explained, "My wife and I vowed that we would treat our children differently than we had been treated when we were young. Because our families told us we could do little right, we virtually had to reconstruct our opinions of ourselves after we met and married. Our philosophy has been to be as positive as we could be with our child. We want him to grow up knowing that he is loved by his mom and dad."

## RATIONALIZATION IS FEAR IN DISGUISE

I had to admire the Walters for their understanding of the errors of their own past and their determination to avoid the same mistakes. Yet I realized, and the Walters came to agree, that they had gone too far in their efforts to be "good" to their children. In an ironic way, they were encouraging Reggie to have a skewed view of himself. He believed that rules would be broken for him. He felt no need to be held accountable for his behavior. His experience had taught him that someone else would take the blame for him whenever he erred. Instead of withholding his feelings as his parents had felt forced to do, he let go of them by blatantly violating the needs of others.

Rationalization is a way of defending ourselves by:

- Justifying the incorrect choices we make.
- Soliciting allies by excusing the mistakes of others.

◆ Temporarily eliminating the probability of conflict with others.
◆ Soothing a conscience that is riddled with guilt.
◆ Denying the existence of complex emotions, such as anger over the past.
◆ Avoiding the need to be immediately accountable for choices we have made.
◆ Proving to ourselves or others that we are open-minded.
◆ Making "payments" for past mistakes.
◆ Preventing feelings from dominating our decisions.

Fear hides behind the mask of rationalization. Typically that fear surrounds the discomfort that accompanies conflict. As the Walters had been taught, many parents feel that only bad things can come from confrontative family interactions. Wanting to stay away from this unacceptable form of communication, parents who rationalize look for ways to make the unacceptable acceptable.

## ❖ THINKING ABOUT YOUR RATIONALE ❖

Parents who consistently rationalize the inappropriate behavior of their children are good at carrying an argument through a logical sequence. The problem is that logical arguments are not always rational. A great argument can be useless if it is based on false assumptions.

Reggie's parents assumed that by giving their son sufficient opportunity to learn from his mistakes he would eventually learn to make wise choices. They gave him every chance to prove he could be counted on to be responsible. Unfortunately, Reggie failed to accept his parents' rational line of thought. Their reliance on faulty reasoning was just the excuse he needed to do as he pleased.

The anxiety that motivates parental rationalization of a child's poor choices can be replaced with confident parental leadership. I find that parents who make excuses for their children are not deliberately setting a child up for failure. Their misguided parental judgment is driven by a hope that the young person will profit from life's experiences. Yet, the nature of the child is such that he does not know which lessons of life he needs to learn. He must be guided by parents who are willing to teach him through the rough experiences life brings.

❖     ❖     ❖

When King Solomon wrote the book of Proverbs, his first few words contain the admonition, "Listen, my son, to your father's instruction and do not forsake your mother's teaching. They will be a garland to grace your head and a chain to adorn your neck."[1] At the outset of this book, Solomon emphasized the parental importance of teaching wisdom and responsibility to a child.

The family responsibility for leadership in teaching wisdom is given to the parents. This requires parents to think beyond the immediate needs of a child. In the place of rationalizing a child's ill-planned behavior is the need to offer him the experiences that lead him to wise conclusions about his responsibility to self and others. The following guidelines are offered to replace the tendency to justify a child's behavior through rationalization:

- Be open to other people's input. Others outside the family may have a more objective view of your child's behavior. The impressions shared by a third party should be seen as valuable information.

- Recall your own youth as you seek to understand your child. Remember that you did not have the wisdom you now possess as a result of your years of experience in life. Your child is inclined to make errors that require adult intervention. It is not safe to assume he will always learn immediately from his mistakes. He needs your help.

- If you are going to make an error, err on the conservative side. It is better to believe your child needs more parental monitoring than to assume he will monitor his own mistakes.

- Endeavor to think as your child thinks. As you put yourself in your child's shoes, you will be more likely to anticipate his motives and behaviors correctly. Gauge your responses to your child's needs according to your understanding of his tendencies.

♦ Be decisive. Many of the choices you must make as a parent are neither totally right nor wrong. Make decisions that reflect the direction you want your family to take. Refrain from second-guessing your decisions. Indecisiveness is a breeding ground for rationalization.

♦ Listen to your "hunches." You know your child better than anyone else. Most of the time your knowledge of his habits will lead you to make the right choice in guiding his behavior.

♦ Recognize the reality that family relationships are an inexact science. You will make mistakes in your decisions on behalf of your child. Be willing to admit your errors to your child, but maintain your resolve to keep your position of family leadership.

We rationalize our child's behavior because we do not want to face the possibility that our child is motivated by intentions that are not honorable. It is normal for parents to want to view their child as being unlikely to do wrong intentionally. In fact, I believe that most of the misguided behaviors children display started out as a well-intentioned effort to communicate some kind of unmet emotional need. Parents who can view their child's behavior objectively are in a position to offer the guidance the child needs to develop responsible behaviors.

# ❖ 9 ❖

# *Understanding Why I Can't Express My Emotions*

**M**rs. Melton was in a quandary. Her four-year-old son, Ryan, would not mind her on their outing to the grocery store. Every time she took her eyes off him, he was into something else. He wanted to touch everything on the shelves. He couldn't understand why he was not allowed to open the boxes his mother had placed in the shopping cart. He begged her to buy whatever looked appealing to him (just about everything in the store).

Mrs. Melton knew the other shoppers were bothered by Ryan's behavior. No one said anything to her, but she could tell by their looks that they thought she should do something about her ill-mannered child. She agreed. She knew she should try to stop her son from being a nuisance to others, but she did not know what to do.

After one of Ryan's loud requests for an item he did not need, Mrs. Melton took him by the arm and spoke calmly to him: "Ryan, you know we don't need that box of cereal. I've already picked out the cereal you like. It's not nice to disobey Mother. Other people are looking at you and asking themselves, 'Why would a sweet boy like that act so ugly toward his mother?' Let's remember our manners. If you're good, we'll do something special when we get home." Mrs.

Melton hoped her appeal would work to quiet her unruly child.

For a moment Ryan's behavior was tolerable. But within a few short minutes, the little guy was busy making life miserable for his mother. As Mrs. Melton selected from a display of apples, she was embarrassed to see Ryan take a big bite out of one of the apples. She knew she had to take action.

Leaning down to Ryan and looking him in the face, Mrs. Melton calmly but firmly said, "Ryan, Mother is getting angry with you. This is the second time I've had to talk to you about your manners. I'm very disappointed in the way you are behaving. When we get home, you'll have to sit by yourself in your bedroom."

Ryan's behavior again improved, but the change was not long-lasting. Mrs. Melton got the items she had to have and determined she would come back to the store later to finish her shopping. She could not stand the tension that accompanied a shopping trip with Ryan.

Later that day, Mrs. Melton talked with a friend about her son's behavior in the grocery store: "Sometimes I don't know what I should do with him. I know he needs to be disciplined, but I don't want to nag him constantly. If I do that, he'll just learn to dislike me." The expression of defeat on her face characterized her spirit at that moment.

Mrs. Melton's more assertive friend took the opportunity to give some unsolicited advice: "I'll tell you what you should do, Jean. The next time he disobeys you, you bust him real hard on the rear end. You do that a few times, and I guarantee he will start acting better when you take him out in public."

Dismissing her friend's words as something she knew she would not do, Jean sighed. "I told Ryan I was angry with him, but that didn't seem to affect him. I don't even think he believed me when I told him." Not only was Ryan unconvinced that his mother felt the way she said she did, deep within, Jean was not really sure of her emotions, either.

## EMOTIONS ARE HIDDEN BEHIND FEAR

Jean's defensive behavior is readily identifiable, but difficult for others to criticize. She talked about her emotion of anger, but was actually fearful of the feeling. She had been taught that most emotions are bad and should be avoided. In place of her true feelings, she attempted to act too friendly. Ryan could see that his mother was upset with him, but her unassertive nature was a signal that he could exploit her to his advantage.

As we view the behavior of people like Jean, it is hard to be critical. Even though unassertive people are not honest in their emotional expression, they are likable. How can someone as nice and gentle as Jean be described in negative terms? Her friend gave her a bit of neighborly advice to be more assertive with her child, but the thought of being emphatic with Ryan was distasteful to her.

## FEELINGS WERE NOT DISCUSSED

Jean was raised in a family where emotions were not handled openly. In fact, the family members did not even discuss their feelings with one another. She told me, "I hardly remember my father getting angry. I think he was afraid to be angry. If he did get upset, my mother would overpower him with her own verbal blast. I realize she was very critical, now that I look back on it. My mother hated it when anyone in our family was angry, but in her mind it was all right for her to express her emotions. I think she sincerely believed she was protecting the family from the harm that might come from constant arguing."

I was interested in what she had learned from her early family life about how to express her own emotions. "I would guess that in the same way your father was afraid to express his emotions, you were also reserved when you wanted to say what you felt."

"Oh, yes! I would have never dreamed of letting my mother know I was mad at her. The tongue-lashings she gave to my dad convinced me I didn't want her to do the same to me. You could say that I was a model child. It wasn't because I wanted to be perfect. I was good because I was scared to be bad."

In this family there was an unspoken rule: *If you feel a negative emotion, you may not express it.* Jean had learned several other false lessons about handling her emotions, including:

- Pretending an emotion does not exist is better than expressing it and being denied your feelings.
- When others express their negative emotions, they do so with the intent to hurt you.

- If you must express your emotions, your expression should be accompanied by an apologetic spirit.
- It is not safe to talk about the way you feel. It is safer to try to change your feelings.
- You should look pleasant on the outside even if you do not feel pleasant inside.
- Broken relationships with others will be difficult to recover if your mood is not always positive.
- If someone else is upset, do all you can to talk them out of their emotions. They do not realize the danger of their feelings.

When she became an adult and entered parenthood, Jean took the lessons from her past and applied them to her own family. Afraid to be anything but nice, she protected herself from her negative feelings by getting rid of them whenever they surfaced. Yet, because she denied herself the freedom to use her emotions in a healthy manner, she was not as effective with her child as she could have been.

Jean told me, "When Ryan misbehaves I almost panic inside. He doesn't know it, but I try hard to be as gentle as I can when I correct him. I want him to learn to respect me as a parent, but I don't want him to feel intimidated by me—the way my family was intimidated by my mother."

I had a good enough rapport with Jean that I could confront her with the discrepancies in her statement: "Jean, I would hazard a guess that Ryan may be aware of how hard you are trying to be gentle toward him. He's not aware that you view angry expressions as a form of intimidation. He does know that he can work on the guilt that is associated with your anger. He can't explain it, but he knows you really don't want to be assertive with him."

Jean was interested in what I had just said, but was not quite sure if she should believe me. "You mean, Ryan is aware of how I feel? How can he be when he doesn't know anything about what his grandmother used to be like when I was a child?"

"He doesn't need to know your personal history. When you tell Ryan you are angry but fail to follow through with assertive action, he sees your words as being empty. He can tell that you are confused about your emotions. He is responding to your confused emotional expression rather than to the words you say." Jean listened with comprehension. I could see the cogs turning in her head.

"You know, when I feel a negative emotion, I freeze inside. I so badly hate being angry that I try hard to block that feeling."

"Let's look at your emotions the way Ryan does. How do you think he perceives you when you're frozen in your emotional expression?" I wanted Jean to carry her thoughts a step further.

"He probably thinks I'm just pretending when I tell him I'm upset with him."

"Is Ryan correct to think that about you?"

Jean laughed. "Probably. It's amazing that a four-year-old child could have a better understanding of how I feel than I have."

## ❖ ALLOWING YOURSELF FREEDOM OF EXPRESSION ❖

Many people, especially those with religious backgrounds, have the misconception that it is not acceptable to be angry. Too many of us have learned that if a "negative" emotion wells up inside, it should be immediately turned into a more positive feeling. Unfortunately, many of our God-given emotions have been so commonly misused that they have gained a negative reputation. At the top of the list is the emotion of anger.

When we look at our human emotions and their usefulness, we find that they can be misused in two ways. The most obvious mishandling of an emotion is in its *overuse*. We can take a good emotion and wear it so that it causes damage in family relationships.

In Jean's family of origin, her mother overused the emotion of anger. She used this emotion to force her husband to submit to her will. She intimidated her children into compliance with the unspoken promise that they would receive the same emotional blast if their behavior was not exemplary. This mother used her emotions in a selfish way. The net result was damage to the atmosphere of the home.

A second way an emotion may be misused is to *ignore* or *under use* it. God made us with the capacity to feel so that we could experience the joys that accompany life itself. In the same way that an overworked emotion creates family discord, emotional neglect can result in unchecked family conflict.

Jean was too quick to dismiss her angry emotions. Her belief that anger is almost always "bad" led her to get rid of this feeling as quickly as she could. By doing so, she excused herself from the God-ordained parental responsibility to provide leadership to her child. She gave lip service to her feelings, but failed to capitalize on the opportunity to correct her son's poor behavioral judgment effectively.

Though unassertive parents rarely intend to send this message, their behavior suggests that they do not care about the emotional needs of their child. The child will accept his parents' lack of assertion as an indication that it is permissible to continue making poor judgments. The young person learns that his parents feel uncomfortable with their feelings. In the same way that the household leaders are confused about how to handle their emotions, the child also grows up confused because he has not been taught proper emotional expression.

Here are some guidelines for healthy emotional expression:

- Be honest with yourself when you experience an emotion. Don't be afraid of those emotions that have been given a bad reputation. They are a part of God's design for you, too.

- Learn to use your emotions as a way to express your love to another person. Affectionate expressions to children include both affirmation and correction.

- Match your outward expressions to your inward feelings. Do not feel forced to smile when you feel angry. Similarly, do not feel obligated to growl when a simple frown will suffice.

- Be completely honest, but also tactful, when you express an emotion. Your family members will know if your emotional utterance is false or if it is genuine.

- Once you have used your emotion to meet its designed purpose, dismiss it. Nothing is more undesirable than an emotion that has overextended its welcome.

◆ Continually evaluate yourself to determine areas in which you need improvement in your emotional expression. Be bluntly honest in your self-evaluation. Be open to the statements others make about you.

One belief Jean and I sought to dispel was that her feelings of anger would do permanent damage to her family if she expressed them. If anything, more damage is done when healthy emotions are left dormant by sidestepping an emotional confrontation just for the sake of temporary peace. This young mother learned to use her emotions as an expression of the commitment she had to her family. She affirmed her child's importance by teaching him how to be responsible to himself and to others.

A concerted effort to understand our emotional makeup allows us to empathize with others. Our knowledge of how we were denied the appropriate use of emotions in the past enables us to reroute emotional expressions from those that are designed to hide feelings to those that promote growth in the family.

CHAPTER

*❖10❖*

# Understanding Why I Fear
# Negative Feelings

B ill and Brittany were at it again. Bill had just taken his younger sister's homework and crumpled it into a ball. "Mom! Bill just ruined my homework! He's trying to tear it up!"

Bill retorted, "I didn't tear it. See, it's all in one piece." He laughed as he uncurled his sister's paper and shook it in her face.

At about the time Bill was taunting Brittany, Mom appeared in the doorway. Quietly she requested Bill to stop aggravating his sister: "Bill, you know that upsets Brittany. Please stop." She took the paper from Bill and handed it to her daughter.

"Brittany, you'll just have to explain to your math teacher what happened. I think she'll understand. I'm not going to make you do it over. That wouldn't be fair to you."

Later that evening, Bill and Brittany were fighting over something else. This time Brittany purposely gave the fish in Bill's aquarium too much food. As he saw his sister pouring the food into the fish tank, Bill screamed, "Stop! You're going to kill my fish!"

Brittany knew she had given the fish much more than they needed, but pleaded ignorance as an excuse for her behavior. "I didn't know how much to give them. They looked hungry to me. Look, they're eating it up."

"You know you're not supposed to give them that much. If you feed them too much, it'll kill them. You did that on purpose!" Bill was angry that his sister had attempted to deceive him.

Rushing into Bill's bedroom to stop the argument between her children, Mom pleaded with the two young people, "Bill, Brittany, please stop that arguing. I don't know what the problem is with you two, but you need to learn to work out your differences without so much fussing."

After briefly scolding the children, Mom conjured a pleasant smile, even though she was not happy with their behavior. Wanting to encourage the children to be mannerly toward one another, she added, "Bill, I want you to give Brittany a hug and tell her you're sorry you yelled at her. And Brittany, I want you to hug Bill because you're sorry you overfed his fish."

The two young people did as their mother instructed, but without enthusiasm. They certainly did not embrace the forgiving attitude that their mother had wanted them to experience.

Once Mom left the room, brother and sister continued their disagreement, but in quieter voices that would not attract their mother's attention. Bill told his sister, "I only hugged you because Mom made me," to make sure she knew his apologetic act was insincere.

As Brenda and I talked about her relationship with her children, she expressed with exasperation, "I do the best I can to keep a positive atmosphere in our home. But it seems that no matter how hard I try to be nice to the children, they never learn. I cringe every time I hear them argue. I want so badly for them to love each other. I always had the dream that my children would grow up being best friends."

Brenda's life had been full of discord and strained relationships. She had never known what family stability meant. Her parents divorced when she was preschool age. For several years, her single mother struggled to make ends meet for her family of three children. When Brenda was nine, her mother remarried. Her new husband was a good provider, but emotionally aloof. He had little to do with Brenda and her siblings and did not seem to be close to Brenda's mother. After three years, the marriage ended.

Soon after the divorce from her second husband, Brenda's

mother married again. This husband was far different from her previous spouse. Loud and argumentative, he dominated the household with his frequent temper outbursts. Though Brenda had not liked her first stepfather, she wished he was back in the house. His passive manner was much easier to tolerate than the new stepfather's abrupt ways.

Brenda recalled the effects her childhood and adolescence had had on her emotional development: "There was never any joy in our home. I remember dreaming about what it must be like to live in a normal home. My mother was always bothered with the chore of raising three children without the support of a loving husband. She was so somber.

"Each time Mother remarried, I got my hopes up, thinking that we'd have a real family. I wanted a home where the parents were happily married and got along really well with the children. Unfortunately, I never had that kind of home. When I married and had children of my own, I hoped that I would always be patient with my children. I planned to discipline them with love rather than by force. I want my children to learn to express their affection openly with one another."

I asked Brenda to assess the success she had achieved in reaching her family goals. She stated sadly, "So far, things haven't worked out as I wanted. When I got married, I thought I was doing the right thing. It turned out, though, that my husband was unfaithful to me. He and I divorced after six years of marriage, leaving me with the sole responsibility of raising our two children. He immediately remarried. I try not to be bitter about the divorce, but I know it has affected the kind of home life my children experience."

## BEING NICE ISN'T ALWAYS BEING RIGHT

Brenda entered marriage and family life with the correct desire to provide emotional warmth for her family. She knew the pain that went along with a family life that was emotionally dead. She came out of her adolescence badly wanting approval. Unsuccessful in satisfying this need in her family of origin, she made experiencing unity a goal for her own family.

Like Brenda, many parents defend themselves from their past by focusing too heavily on the positive and ignoring their negative

feelings. This parenting style is similar to the unassertive characteristic we viewed earlier. Parents may take on the role of the "nice
guy" because of unmet childhood needs for affection. A parenting
style based on this need is characterized by the following:

- Passive tendencies are strong. There is a fear that asser-
  tiveness suggests a lack of love.
- The tendency to look for strengths in others is so strong
  that the need to give attention to weaknesses is ignored.
- The natural flow of emotions is blocked. Only positive emotions are allowed expression.
- Confrontation is feared, even though the situation may call
  for such an encounter.
- Obvious signs of trouble within the family are disregarded
  in the hope that trouble spots will disappear.
- Suppressed negative feelings become so strong that a sense
  of despair develops.

## POSITIVE EFFORTS MAY HAVE NEGATIVE RESULTS
In an interesting way, the attempts of the parents to force a positive
atmosphere on the home can have an opposite effect. A child may
recognize her parents' attempts always to be positive as an opportunity to manipulate the home environment to her advantage.

At Brenda's request, I saw Bill and Brittany together so I could
gain an understanding of their view of the family. As they talked of
the atmosphere in the home, it quickly became evident that they
used their mother's well-intentioned parenting as an opportunity to
take charge of the household. They knew she did not want to be firm
with them and took advantage of the opportunity to set their own
rules of conduct.

Here are several of the statements Bill and Brittany made about
their home atmosphere:

- "Mom gives us several chances to act right before she
  makes us be good."
- "We know that we probably won't be punished when she
  says we will be."
- "Mom is always willing to let us make a deal with her."

- "When we cry, Mom usually gives in. She hates to see us act sad."
- "Mom tells us we've been good, even though we know we haven't."

These statements told a lot about the lessons Brenda had learned earlier in her life. Brenda grew up without the affirmation needed to cause her to feel good about her family relationships. In her adulthood, she went too far to ensure a positive home climate, which gave her children the chance to wreck the atmosphere of the home.

Brenda had hoped her children would recognize and appreciate her attempt to be as upbeat as she possibly could. Instead, the young people recognized her yielding nature as an opportunity to act however they pleased.

### ❖ USING CONFRONTATION TO SHOW LOVE ❖

One of the most difficult tasks, I believe, for many parents is to understand when to confront a child with firmness and when to show a kind and forgiving spirit. It may be simple to display positive emotions, such as happiness, forgiveness, acceptance, or love. But emotions such as anger, guilt, worry, or impatience are more difficult to know how to use effectively.

Brenda felt it was wrong to be impatient with her children. She thought that a lack of patience would also convey a lack of acceptance. Yet, in time she learned that she could place realistic demands on her children without the irritability that so often accompanies an impatient nature. As she asserted herself in her children's presence, they learned to view her lack of tolerance for misbehavior as a positive sign of parental love.

I challenged Brenda to ask herself a number of questions about the way she used her emotions to control the atmosphere of her home. Her responses to these questions told her whether or not she was actually creating the positive home environment that had evaded her during her childhood. These questions include:

- What do you hope to gain through positive emotions?
- How do your family members interpret the way you act

and the feelings you show?
- ◆ Does your outward behavior match the feelings you have within?
- ◆ How do your family members indicate that your words and emotions do not match?
- ◆ What lessons did you learn from your past about negative emotions?
- ◆ Can you recognize that good can be found in properly expressing emotions we consider to be negative?
- ◆ What happens to the emotions you fail to express?
- ◆ Are your family members more aware of your moods than you are?
- ◆ In what ways can a negative atmosphere result from trying too hard to be positive?

As we understand the design God has for humankind, we can more fully comprehend the role our emotions play in creating a healthy family life. God made men and women with the capacity to feel a wide range of emotions. He also made all of us with the capacity to understand the positive uses of each of our emotions. The experiences of life provide the greatest, and sometimes most painful, lessons about our responsibility to those we love.

Brenda assumed that she should not express any emotion that would convey to her children any hint of mistrust or doubt. Her past experiences convinced her that the absence of warmth, respect, affection, and praise creates a home atmosphere that results in repeated defeat for the family.

I explained to Brenda that she was exactly right in her assumption. She should simply add to her beliefs the need to hold her children accountable for their behavior since their youth prevented them from making wise decisions consistently. Her negative childhood experiences had thrust her into an imbalanced way of attending to her family's emotional needs.

Think about these words: "Do not conform any longer to the pattern of this world, but be transformed by the renewing of your mind. Then you will be able to test and approve what God's will is—his good, pleasing and perfect will."[1] We often learn inappropriate lessons of life, and miss the perfect intention God has for our lives.

Our past experiences may have taught us, as they taught Brenda, to use our emotions incorrectly as a way of controlling the emotional tempo of the home. The Bible gives us hope for a positive reversal of this cycle. By understanding God's design for the family we can show firm leadership while also creating a positive home atmosphere.

# ❖11❖

# *Understanding Why*
# *I Overpower My Child*

"**O**scar! Get in here right this minute!" Dad's voice bellowed through the entire house. Oscar had no trouble understanding the urgency of his father's request. He dreaded what he knew would be an unpleasant encounter, but he dared not disobey the command to enter his father's presence.

"Yes, sir?" Oscar was the picture of meekness, but beneath his subservient outward appearance was an unspoken anger. He hated to be talked to in the demeaning style that was so typical of his father.

"What's this I hear about you talking back to your mother?" Dad glared at his son, waiting for an answer. Before he spoke, Oscar already knew that no answer would be good enough for his father. The boy felt trapped.

"I wasn't talking back, Dad," explained the intimidated boy. "I was just. . . ."

"I don't want to hear any of your excuses! You weren't 'just' doing anything. You were being disrespectful to your mother, and you know it! Polite boys do not tell their mother that they refuse to cooperate.

It's my understanding that you told your mother you wouldn't take out the trash after she asked you for the third time to do it. I call that disrespectful behavior!"

Oscar tried one more time to reason with his father: "But Dad, I didn't say I wouldn't take out the trash. I said I wanted to wait until this TV show was over. I was going to take it out in just a few minutes." Oscar could tell by the look on his father's face he had not done an effective job of convincing him to see things his way.

"I don't care if that TV show has only one minute left! When your mother tells you to do something, you do it! Have I made myself clear?" Oscar nodded. "You get the trash, and take it out right now. Then go straight to your room. You're grounded for the rest of the day!"

Oscar dutifully performed the assigned task and slowly made his way to his bedroom. His brother had heard the clash between Oscar and their dad. He was glad he had not been the object of his father's wrath, but felt some empathy toward his sibling.

"Hey, Oscar, are you okay?"

"Shut up."

"I'm just being nice. I heard Dad yelling at you. You have to stay in here the rest of the night?" Oscar refused to respond to the solace his brother offered. He sat quietly and sulked. Inwardly he wondered why his father was always so overbearing.

❖   ❖   ❖

Oscar's father, Mr. Gradel, defended his behavior to himself by believing that he was doing only what was best for his sons. He did not enjoy being forceful with his children, but was convinced that to be passive would allow them to build bad habits. He explained his gruff ways as a necessity of family life. Unless he strongly impressed on his children the need to submit to authority, they would grow up to be disrespectful of others' needs. He was willing to sacrifice popularity to ensure that his children develop proper manners.

Mr. Gradel had grown up in a family that he described as "much more argumentative than my family has ever thought of being." His father was the central figure. Nothing happened that he did not know about. If any decision needed to be made, it went through the father.

He was completely in command of his household.

I listened one day as Mr. Gradel told me of his recollections of his childhood: "When I was a boy I would not have dared talk back to my parents the way my children do to me. I knew that if I did I would catch a backhand across my face. My father was the boss of our family, and I did not challenge him."

As Mr. Gradel talked further of his father, it became clear that he had few feelings of affection for the man. "My father was not the kind of man who would pat you on the back or tell you what a good job you had done. He assumed you could conclude for yourself whether or not your effort was your best. He was not comfortable being affectionate. That simply wasn't his style. It was hard for me to feel close to my father, but I have to admit I learned a lot about being responsible. No one can accuse me of being unreliable."

As Mr. Gradel told me of his family background, I was interested in the effects of his father's nature on Mr. Gradel's ability to show affection toward his own family. "I guess that's not my strong suit. I know I need to be more affectionate toward my sons . . ." pondered Mr. Gradel as his voice tapered off. It seemed that he was recalling childhood experiences that led him to become a hard and controlling father.

It became evident that Mr. Gradel was defending himself against feelings of anger toward his own upbringing. He did not like the fact that he was gruff and difficult for his children to like. He had not been taught to be tender and affirming with his children. The only way he knew to influence his family was by means of force. He had come to accept that he may have to sacrifice his relationship with his sons in order to give them the instruction they needed to learn to interact effectively in this world.

## POWER WAS MISUSED IN CHILDHOOD

We express our behaviors for a wide variety of reasons. The power plays of one adult can be motivated by different reasons than those that drive another. I find that overpowering parents are reacting to two sources of simmering dissatisfaction: (1) a reaction to the loss of control experienced earlier in life; (2) the inability to express feelings of affection comfortably.

When Mr. Gradel was a child he had limited opportunity to

express his emotions. In fact, he stated that while his behavior during his youth was exemplary, he rarely had the chance to state what he felt. He never talked back to his father, did not openly second-guess his father's decisions, and always complied with his father's demands, no matter how trivial they seemed.

Though Mr. Gradel could have been described in his youth as compliant and well-behaved, he harbored feelings of resentment for the stronghold his father had over his emotions. As a boy he had been told, "If you have any feelings, you had better keep them to yourself." For years, this young person was unable to state his emotions honestly.

Fatherhood marked for Mr. Gradel the opportunity to express feelings of anger, which had been forced within during his earlier years. Now that his father was no longer around to dominate him, Mr. Gradel could elevate himself to the position of control he had never been allowed to occupy in his youth. He now had the chance to make decisions that would be authoritative. And he was going to make the most of his opportunity.

One way a parent defends his overpowering tendencies is to believe that one day he will be admired for his position of control. Mr. Gradel's hope was, "Someday my children will look back on their childhood experiences and be thankful I was demanding of them. They may dislike the things I am trying to teach them, but I'm building character in them. They don't appreciate me now, but they will later in life."

The overpowering parent often comes out of a background in which he felt little appreciation. During childhood, he did not feel as though he was admired for anything but the capacity to be dominated. Unmet needs of affirmation can deceive the adult into believing that admiration can be gained by taking on the role of the family general.

## NEVER LEARNED TO EXPRESS TENDER EMOTIONS
Perhaps a more pitiable result of Mr. Gradel's childhood was his lack of opportunity to learn to express tender emotions. He told me, "My father showed me he loved me by being tough on me. He wanted me to be prepared to face the difficulties life brings." In the process of being trained to confront crisis situations, Mr. Gradel had lost his

ability to relate to others emotionally.

Mr. Gradel used the same explanation for his own power tactics: "I'm tough on my kids because I'm looking out for their best interests." In actuality, his statement should have been, "I'm tough on my kids because I'm afraid to express my emotions." Having learned that emotions have no place in a man's world, Mr. Gradel had become fearful of the feelings that were a part of his personality makeup.

The overpowering parent assumes that a show of emotions equates a loss of personal control. Past experiences often convince the adult that unless total control of the family environment is achieved, the threat of childhood rebellion will be realized. The overpowering tendencies of a parent include:

- An unwillingness to listen to the thoughts and opinions of family members.
- Holding on to personal opinions without feeling the need to examine their accuracy periodically.
- Intimidating others through threat, coercion, or actual force.
- Withholding emotions, since emotional expressions represent opportunities for others to manipulate their way into the position of control.
- Dismissing a child's feelings as a byproduct of his immaturity.
- Convincing oneself that in time the child will be appreciative of the power structure of the home.
- An unwillingness to compromise for fear of appearing to be weak.
- A tendency to judge family "happiness" by the compliance of the children rather than by the relationships among family members.

## ❖ DISCARDING DOMINATION ❖

The irony in the behavior of the overbearing parent is in the fact that, by pushing decisions on a child, the parent is actually losing his position of importance in that child's life. A child who feels overpowered by his parent frequently will head in the opposite direction when he gets out from under that controlling hand.

❖          ❖          ❖

In the Bible's short book of Zechariah, the author writes to the Jews who were held in exile from their homeland. Zechariah directs a comment to the leaders of the Jewish people as they look toward the monumental task of rebuilding the temple in Jerusalem. In the most well-known verse in this otherwise obscure book, God states that it will be "not by might nor by power, but by my Spirit" that powerful deeds will be accomplished.[1]

All those in positions of leadership, including parents, can apply those words of wisdom. When we acknowledge our parental position as a designation from God, we become free from the need to force control over others. Overpowering behavior typically results from a need to satisfy our own unmet needs and desires.

Finding assurance that we are secure in our spiritual position of importance in the eyes of God leads us to set aside the compulsion to address personal shortcomings from our past. A personal attitude of cooperation gives us freedom in relationships. Overpowering adults are governed by the insecurities of their past. Without change as adults, they are destined to continue in the frustration they experienced in relationships as children.

# ❖12❖

# *Understanding Why I Can't Face Reality*

M rs. Ketchum sat with her head buried in her hands. She wanted, in the worst way, to get out of the conversation she was having with her fifteen-year-old daughter. She felt trapped. Her daughter was harshly complaining, "Mother, you are blind! Doug has never been nice to me. He has always treated me like a stepdaughter. I've known from the day he married you that he didn't want me to be part of his life."

Mrs. Ketchum stopped her daughter: "Now wait just a minute, Marla. 'Never' and 'always' are pretty strong words. I don't think you can say Doug *never* treats you nice or that he is *always* mean to you. You're not being fair. You have to start being realistic about our family and quit talking like you know what Doug feels about you. You can't read his mind."

Marla had plenty she wanted to say: "Mother, I think I know what Doug thinks about me. How could a man who loves his step-daughter suggest that she's 'easy' with boys?"

Mrs. Ketchum interrupted abruptly: "You wait just a minute! Doug never said anything like that. You take that statement back, young lady!"

"He most certainly did! You were sitting right beside him when he said it. When I went to Jimmy's last week, Doug said he knew that we both had only one thing on our minds. And when I told him that was totally wrong, he just said, 'Yeah, right.' How am I supposed to take that?"

Mrs. Ketchum would not give up her hope of convincing Marla that Doug was not the villain she depicted him to be. "Marla, you don't realize how much Doug has done for you. He only wants to help you when he says things like that. He wants to be a father-figure to you, but you won't give him a chance!"

"Oh, well, I guess that explains why he hits me. He thinks that's what a loving father-figure is supposed to do." Marla's voice held a strong tone of sarcasm as she verbally taunted her mother.

"He does not *hit* you, Marla. He slaps you. You have no idea what it means to be hit." As those words came out of her mouth, Mrs. Ketchum started to cry.

Mrs. Ketchum's own experience convinced her that Marla was far more fortunate than she realized. Mrs. Ketchum knew what it meant to be abused by a stepfather. When she was in elementary school, her parents divorced and her mother remarried a man who could be described only in the worst terms. He was an alcoholic and thought nothing of spending his weekly paycheck on beer rather than on household bills. When this man was drunk, his usual foul mood became unbearable. He cursed everybody in sight and thought nothing of beating his wife or the children.

Mrs. Ketchum told me of the horrors she experienced: "I remember that I dreaded the weekends. That was when my stepfather drank the most. He drank all during the week, but not as much as on the weekend. He would come home drunk and in a terrible mood. We were all afraid of him. We never knew which one of us would be the target for his rage."

"Those years must have been a hard test of endurance for you and your family." I refrained from further comment, wanting Mrs. Ketchum to continue with her thoughts.

"When I was a teenager I didn't want to believe that my stepfather was abusing me and my family. I hated him, but I thought that admitting I was abused somehow made me dirty. I just pretended that life would eventually get better. I believed in myself and convinced myself that my adult years would be happy. I was a survivor.

"The thing I don't understand about Marla is that she thinks she can change her stepfather. I know he's hard on her, but she really doesn't know what it's like to have a mean stepfather. I wish she could see what life was like in my family. She'd be a lot more appreciative of our current family life if she knew how bad it could be."

The only way Mrs. Ketchum got through her teenage years was to daydream about the future. In a sense, she could not be faulted for denying the awful realities of her family life with an abusive and alcoholic stepfather. Certainly, her denial prevented her from facing life's reality at the time, but it also protected her, in a sense, from constant despair.

Mrs. Ketchum could be faulted for holding on to her coping mechanism beyond its usefulness. She wanted Marla to escape confrontation with her childhood and adolescent fears in the same way. Marla got this message loud and clear. At one point the teenager complained to me, "My mother wants me to just sit back and take it from Doug, the same way she did from her stepfather. She wants me to pretend that my emotions aren't there."

DENIAL MAY BE MASKED

Denial takes a variety of forms. The most obvious type of denial is simply to turn the other direction and refuse to acknowledge that a circumstance is present. A person may engage in denial in other ways:

- Pretending that, by leaving matters alone, things will get better.
- Blaming oneself for the actions of another person.
- Accepting the distorted interpretations of others who are engaged in denial.
- Making excuses for those who do damage to the family.
- Making promises to self or others to be assertive, but then failing to follow through.
- Taking out feelings of anger on someone other than the person who is responsible for those feelings.
- Expressing feelings of emotional hurt through irresponsible behavior.

Mrs. Ketchum's denial led her into a marriage that closely mirrored her mother's marriage years earlier. Since Mrs. Ketchum had used fantasies to cope with a bad family situation, rather than confronting the reality of her grim youth and learning from it, she found history repeating itself in her adult family experiences.

Marla helped Mrs. Ketchum recognize the similarities between the relationships of their current family and of her past. "Mother, let me tell you what I think about how Doug compares to your step-father. Both men are opinionated. Neither likes to be embarrassed by someone else—especially someone young like me. Both fly off the handle easily. They say that they are being hard on someone out of love, but I think they really just want to be in charge. Both of them have an awful temper and say anything that comes to mind. Only one thing about Doug isn't the same as your stepfather—he doesn't drink."

Mrs. Ketchum summarized this conversation to me by saying, "I had to admit that a lot of what Marla said was true. I had always thought that since Doug was not an alcoholic, somehow all his other qualities were much easier to accept. In my mind, if a man does not drink and is not physically abusive, he isn't that bad."

## PAST DENIAL MUST BE FACED

As Mrs. Ketchum began to view her past with greater understanding, Marla was able to communicate more effectively with her. She had not intended to stymie her communication with Marla, but her unwillingness to see both her past and present family life realistically kept her emotionally distant from her daughter.

Several thoughts are found in the minds of those who use denial as a shield from the pains of the past and the present. These thoughts are so dominant that they dictate the behaviors of the denying adult. They include:

- If I show how I really feel, the power of my negative emotions will ruin my relationships with those I love.
- The strength of my positive thinking will overcome the negative impact of our family's reality.
- If I love someone, I have to encourage them in all they do, in spite of their personal flaws.

- ◆ Confrontation of our family's faults will only make matters worse.
- ◆ Maybe the rest of the family won't be as badly affected by our family's turmoil as I fear.
- ◆ If I confront the problems of our family, I may be labeled by other family members as a troublemaker.
- ◆ If I reveal my true feelings, I'm afraid I would do more damage than good, so I'd better keep my thoughts to myself.
- ◆ It's better that I be forgiving of others in the family rather than openly express my emotions.

Mrs. Ketchum and I examined the ways she viewed her family relationships. She came to realize that her behavior was motivated by beliefs that convinced her to ignore reality. Her mistaken hope was that by disregarding problems, they would simply go away. She admitted, "You know, I've been living under the assumption all these years that if I just show enough patience, life will get better. If Marla had not pointed out how I hide from difficulties, I would never have looked within myself and learned how I really feel. I could have waited forever for life to take a sudden change for the better."

## DENIAL MAY BE INTERPRETED AS A LACK OF LOVE
During one of our meetings, Marla said something to her mother that stunned her: "Mother, if you loved me you'd try to understand the way I feel. You don't have to agree with me. I just want you to understand me."

Mrs. Ketchum was floored by the suggestion that she did not love her child. "Marla, I love you more than I love my own life. You don't really mean that you think I don't love you, do you?" Marla simply shrugged her shoulders.

Marla's statement caused Mrs. Ketchum to examine carefully the way she showed love, or denied it, to her daughter. She had previously assumed that Marla recognized her peacekeeping role in the family as evidence of her affection. This adult had been living under the incorrect assumption that by withholding her feelings, she was sending a message of devotion to the family.

Not consumed by the same thoughts, Marla interpreted her

mother's denial of their family's problems as a sign that her mother did not love her at all. Though she could not give precise terminology to her mother's emotions, she recognized her mother to be dependent on a lifestyle that provided her with security, even if that security was unhealthy.

Through her denial, Mrs. Ketchum hoped to avoid making waves in the family. But, she realized that she could show her love to Marla and her husband by doing the very thing she feared—making waves. Her newfound ability to stand up to her family's problems effectively killed her dependent relationship to a man who was deficient in relationship skills. To her surprise, it opened the door for healing in a family that needed renewed strength.

### ❖ MAKING FORGIVENESS AN ACTION WORD ❖

Many of us have a tendency to believe that to be forgiving also requires a passive spirit of acceptance. Such a concept creates a breeding ground for the denial of feelings. It prevents good from coming out of a seemingly negative situation.

Certainly, Mrs. Ketchum wanted to be forgiving of those who had done damage to family relationships. Yet, by failing to act on her emotions, she allowed family damage to continue unchecked. Her denial of the need to confront her family's cycle of abuse caused Marla to assume that she was unloved.

We can see in the very life of the Lord Jesus that it is right to be forgiving while simultaneously confronting the harm caused by human error. He taught us that when we pray we should request forgiveness.[1] Yet, He also showed His willingness to be assertive toward those who provoke harm.[2]

Our denial is often prompted by feelings of compassion that have been overworked. Believing that a compassionate person would not directly confront another with the disturbing facts of reality, many are duped into withholding their emotions. Their belief is that by denying the need to demand accountability in addition to offering forgiveness, life's events will eventually work toward a positive end.

Mrs. Ketchum truly believed that by giving her husband a vote of support with no expectations attached to his role in the family, he would recognize her faith in him and respond with responsible behavior. Instead, he saw her as dependent on his erring lifestyle and took advantage of her unassertiveness by being abusive.

Jesus' show of anger was a statement of His disagreement with the distortions that were in the minds of others who were self-centered. He saw people in need who were being denied their very dignity. Rather than deny the reality before Him, Jesus took action and corrected negative circumstances. His assertive acts were motivated by His compassion for the human soul.

As we look to rid ourselves of the tendency to deny the grim realities of failing family circumstances, we should ask several questions to determine the effects of our leadership choices on our children:

- Do I understand the boundaries of my emotions?
- Do I use my emotions effectively, or do I use them to hide from the difficult circumstances of my family life?
- What does it take for me to become angry?
- What do I do with my feelings of internal discomfort?
- Have I become hardened to the effects of others' behavior on my children?
- Am I afraid to be honest about the way my child interprets family relationships?
- Do I recognize that compassion for others allows me to confront obvious behavioral and attitudinal flaws?

# PART
# 3

## PARENTING THE WAY
## YOU WISH YOU'D
## BEEN PARENTED

❖

Mr. Knight told me, "When I look at my friends' children, I sometimes wonder why they don't act the way Reynolds does. I can't really
understand what it is about my home that causes my son to be so
belligerent. Sure, other kids test their parents, but they aren't as
difficult to handle as Reynolds. A lot of times I have thought his
behavior problems are all my fault. I wonder what it is I do that
causes him to seem to hate me so much."

Mr. Knight wanted what every good parent wants for his children. He loved his son dearly, but had lost his ability to exercise the
kind of influence over the boy that would prevent him from getting
into such trouble. Confused and worried, he had come to my office
hoping to find direction for his family.

❖   ❖   ❖

There are a number of factors I consider to be important in shaping
the atmosphere of a home, but two stand out as being most important. The first is the way the parents' personalities give shape to the
behavior of the child. The second is the reaction the child offers to his
parents as a result of his own personality.

I have heard many parents say something like this: "I try to treat my children the same. One of my children seems to accept this, while the other totally rejects my efforts at discipline. I'm confused about how to interpret this difference. I don't know if I should try to force my 'problem' child to accept the way I do things, or if I should cater to her and treat her differently."

The parent is the leader of the home. An obligation, then, of the family leader is to make decisions that are in the best interest of all family members. These decisions must be based on a thorough knowledge of both the child's inborn nature and the temperament you, as the family leader, bring into the home.

There are two gifts each parent should give to himself. The first is the gift of knowing your child so completely that you can anticipate and understand his moods and behaviors. The second gift is to understand yourself in such a complete way that you know the strengths and weaknesses you bring into your family relationships.

Regardless of the type of home you came from, you have acquired both good habits and bad habits as you learned to get along with others. The good news is that as an adult you have the capacity to look back on your past with an understanding you did not possess in your youth. That understanding can propel you to make the adjustments needed to make your family life more rewarding.

I have learned through my work with families and through my experiences with my own family that being willing to continually adjust to the needs of our children strengthens us as family leaders. We will see behaviors in our children that give us great insight into the changes we, as parents, need to make on their behalf. I will examine several of the more common ways parents may see themselves in their child's behavior. My hope is that, by understanding the communication of our children, we can also understand more about our need to adjust the lessons we may have learned from the past.

# ❖13❖

# *Exchanging Mistrust*
# *for Trust*

H al and his father had agreed that Hal would trim the hedges in the back yard for fifteen dollars. Dad was par- ticular about the way he wanted the job done and care- fully went over the details with Hal. Hal did not enjoy his father's perfectionistic ways and was less than enthusiastic as he agreed to do the job according to Dad's standards.

"Okay, Dad. I know what to do. Just let me get it over with so I can get the money." There was a haughty tone in Hal's voice that his father did not like.

Feeling the need to warn his son, Dad added as he walked into the house, "Remember, if you want the fifteen dollars, it has to be done right. I won't accept a job that's only partially done." Hal mut- tered to himself as he began trimming the hedge.

After Hal was convinced he had completed the chore to his father's specifications, he went inside the house and summoned his father to inspect his work. He hoped his dad would quickly agree that the job was complete and give him the money.

Instead of quickly looking over Hal's efforts, Dad made his way around the yard, carefully inspecting Hal's work. "This looks good,

Hal. You've done a nice job. Just one more thing before I pay you. I'd like you to cut the dead branch off that bush over there and carry it to the curb so the trash collector can take it away. It won't take you long."

At that moment Hal felt he could justify a complaint against his father. He had not committed to cutting off any dead limbs from the hedges. He felt his father was trying to force him to do more work than they had agreed on. "But Dad, you didn't tell me I'd have to do that. I'm only getting paid to trim the hedges, not cut off dead limbs. That's not fair!" He stood firmly beside his father, but failed to make eye contact.

"Hal, it won't take you a minute to cut off that limb. Besides, it will make your job look much better. It doesn't look right to have a dead branch among these neatly trimmed hedges. I'll give you the money once that's done."

Hal did not want to give in to his father. He thought that this was just another in a long line of instances in which his father took advantage of him. Complaining, he said, "I knew when you told me you'd pay me to trim the hedges, you'd add something else. You're always trying to get me to do more than I'm supposed to do."

An argument ensued, with father and son each accusing the other. Hal said his father was breaking his agreement to pay him for a specific job. He thought his father was manipulative. Dad was angry because of his son's unwillingness to go even one step beyond the boundaries of the task he had been given. He argued that Hal was ungrateful and insensitive and exhibited a bad attitude. He felt justified in the comments he made.

As the two argued, Dad became increasingly upset. Finally unable to stand any more of his son's smart talk, he verbally leveled the young person: "Listen to me, young man! If you think for a minute that I'm going to take this kind of talk from you, you'd better think again. I'm sick and tired of your whining and complaining. All you ever do is think of yourself. You never consider what you could do to help out around here. That kind of attitude isn't going to get you anywhere in life. You're going to be told repeatedly in life that your work wasn't quite as thorough as you thought, so get used to it!"

With that verbal explosion, Dad stood guard as Hal did the additional work. Both father and son wore a scowl. After the chore was complete, Hal looked expectantly at his father for his money. Knowing his son's thoughts, Dad turned away from him and curtly stated, "I haven't decided yet if you deserve to be paid."

## PENT-UP EMOTIONS WILL ERUPT

Hal's actual concern was not that he had to add five minutes of additional work to his assigned chore. He felt contempt for the way his father failed to consider his needs as he forced another job on him without also offering additional pay. Though Hal's father accused him of being insensitive to the requests of others, Hal felt the same label could be applied to his dad. The moment Dad requested that Hal add just a little more to the job he had been assigned, Hal seized the opportunity to vent stored-up emotions against his father.

Dad had every right to feel annoyed at Hal's complaint that he was being overworked, for certainly he was not. Yet the verbal shower of criticism that thundered over Hal gives a strong hint at why he chose to question his father's authority. Instead of accepting Hal's criticism and politely negotiating, Dad allowed the conversation to deteriorate into an assault on the young person's character.

Hal implied that his dad was trying to cheat him out of a few extra dollars for more work. Dad simultaneously felt Hal was holding too tightly to his agreement and was, in essence, trying to cheat by refusing to budge from the letter of their unwritten contract. In actuality, Hal was using the dispute as an opportunity to voice an ongoing complaint. Knowing of no other way to tell his dad that he was too quick to stretch his expectations of others, he tried to slip his request for greater consideration into this chance to complain.

## REVENGE IS SWEET—DECADES TOO LATE

After the argument, neither Hal nor his dad felt proud or pleased at their altercation. Hal was upset that his father had missed the point of his reluctance to do the extra work. Dad was disheartened that he had felt forced to put his apparently insensitive son in his proper place.

In an odd way, however, Dad felt a certain justification for his chosen reaction to his son. As a boy, he had lived under the harsh rule of his father and mother. Neither of his parents would allow him to step outside the boundaries of disciplined behavior they expected of him. He felt as a young person that he was unfortunate enough to have the strictest parents of any of his friends.

This man's reaction to his upbringing was to develop a perfectionistic approach to tasks. He learned that in order to stay out from under the criticism of his parents, it was best simply to do a job right the first time. He did not like the fact that he was shown no leniency from his parents, but he learned that to try to make them budge from their set ways was useless.

In a cyclical pattern, Dad had acquired many of the qualities as an adult he disliked in his parents as a youth. He was demanding of his children and expected them to live up to certain high standards. When his children questioned his tendency to require them to do more than what was clearly expected, he took the opportunity to blast them into compliance. The force of his expression to Hal was in many ways equal to the strength of his own dislike for the methods his strict parents had used as they raised him.

As a child, Dad had never been allowed the opportunity to express his opinions to his parents, especially those that contained criticism. As an adult, he took advantage of the chance to vent his sentiments to his family, even if it meant stepping on the tender needs of his children in the process. Though it was not clear to Hal, his father's demand for absolute perfection marked the adult's need to gain a degree of revenge for being denied the chance to express his emotions during his youth.

### ❖ THE GIFT OF TRUST ❖

As Hal complained to his father about having to complete extra work, he was asking for a reason to trust in others and in himself. His father's tendency to squeeze a little more work out of him than was originally expected sent a message to Hal. Hal believed he could not trust his father to be completely honest in his intentions with him. He also received the suggestion that the work he did was never quite good enough.

By saying, "But Dad, you didn't tell me I'd have to do that. . . . That's not fair!" Hal sent a simple message to his father in disguised fashion. Through his complaint, he stated, "Dad, I believe you have

wronged me again. I am pointing this out with the hope that it can
be corrected."

Let's go back to that point in this father-son interaction and
change the response given to Hal. Instead of reacting in a way
that quickly led to a verbal attack on an apparently ungrateful
son, Dad could have given any of a number of alternative responses,
including:

- "You're right. What kind of adjustment do you think we
  should make on our agreement?"
- "You're ready for this job to be over, aren't you?"
- "I'll tell you what, let's do this extra job together. It's only
  fair that I help you."
- "Remind me to buy you a milkshake the next time we go out
  for a hamburger to make up for the extra time you spend."
- (chuckles) "I'll bet you think I'm a hard person to please."

Dad could have made any of the above statements to his disheartened son. The likelihood is strong that Hal would have left the
conversation with the feeling that his father could be trusted to see
matters his way. In an interesting way, he then would have been
more likely to assume responsibility for coming to the conclusions
his father tried to force on him. He would be open to conclude any
of the following:

- My dad recognizes the hard work I do. I am a capable
  person.
- I shouldn't expect extra pay for just a few minutes work,
  especially from someone who appreciates my effort.
- I want to extend myself to others the way they are willing
  to extend themselves to me.
- It feels good to know that my dad understands me. I want
  to cooperate with him.

In his youth, Dad was never given the opportunity to feel the
confidence of his parents. Their frequent criticisms left him with
the belief that people could not be fully trusted. He concluded that
it was always in his best interest to stay in an aggressive position in

his relationships. By asking for just a little more than was necessary, he kept the upper hand in his relationships.

Dad could break that cycle by demonstrating to his son a trust that had not been shown him. His gracious acceptance of his son's feelings could allow Hal to assume a more positive approach to relationships.

❖   ❖   ❖

One root of faith in God is the willingness to place trust in our worth as one of God's valued creations. King David expressed his awe that humankind is placed at the top of all God's creations.[1] This recognition of his personal value in God's eyes encouraged David to write, "Trust in the LORD. . . . Commit your way to the LORD; trust in him."[2] David had learned that, as the climax of God's creation, his life could be marked by the confidence that comes with the belief that his value was secure.

The concepts of trust, security, and worth are taught primarily through the relationship a child has with his parents. As a child is taught that he can express all his emotions freely, he will learn that he can trust his world. He will have faith in those who guide him. He will be open to relationships that require both give and take.

CHAPTER

## ❖14❖

# *Exchanging Unhappiness for Satisfaction*

A beautiful fifteen-year-old girl sat in my office crying as she told me of her constant feelings of unhappiness. Looking down at the floor, she said, "Nobody knows how unhappy I am. They all think I'm this bubbly little girl who has everything going for her."

I knew what Gina was talking about and responded, "On the outside it seems that you have everything a girl could want. There's hardly anything you don't have."

"That's just it," the teen continued. "I don't see why I'm so unhappy all the time. What do you think?"

I sat silently as Gina thought about her question. I knew it was important that she understand what she thought about her unhappiness. Looking up, she asked another question: "Do you think I'm spoiled?" I smiled faintly, acknowledging that I did feel she had been spoiled by her giving parents.

Gina answered her own question: "I *know* I'm spoiled. I think that's half my problem." By now she had quit crying and was trying to understand her emotions.

"Explain what you mean," I encouraged.

"I mean, I've gotten everything I ever wanted since I was a little girl."

"And you think that's not so good?"

Gina thought for a moment and smiled. "I'm not saying I want to give everything back. But I know I've been given too much."

Wanting Gina to comprehend more about her feelings of unhappiness, I stated, "Somehow being spoiled and being unhappy seem related." I waited for the girl's response.

Instead of responding directly to my statement, Gina asked me another question: "Do you think I'm selfish?" Again I waited, knowing I did not need to react verbally. Almost immediately Gina answered herself, "I probably am selfish."

"So being spoiled can lead to being selfish, which can lead to being unhappy," I summarized the thoughts she had expressed. I could see Gina making sense out of her emotions.

I later met separately with Gina's parents. They wanted to know more of their role in helping their daughter overcome her unhappiness. Mr. Vickers smiled as he stated, "Gina tells us she's learned that she is selfish and spoiled. We've known that for a long time. We're glad she's finally figuring it out for herself. I guess maybe we have spoiled her."

I reacted by acknowledging, "There are times when we think we are doing what is right for our children, but later we find that our good intentions have backfired. I doubt that you gave special attention to Gina with the intent of making her unhappy."

Mr. and Mrs. Vickers nodded. Mrs. Vickers offered her thoughts: "When Gina was little, she was such an easy child to dote on. I had wanted a little girl in the worst way, and I guess I went too far in making sure her life was easy."

"Where did things go wrong?" My question was intended to help these parents look for adjustments that could be made on Gina's behalf.

Mrs. Vickers answered, "I place a lot of the blame on myself. Steve warned me when Gina was young that I was making a spoiled brat out of her. I had never had that kind of attention when I was young, and I wanted to make sure my daughter knew she was special. So, to show her she was special, I gave her whatever I could and bent most of the rules for her. She seemed appreciative. I'm not quite sure when the tide began to turn, but I think it's safe to say that by the time she was a teenager, I knew I had a child who was hard to live with."

## THE MAKING OF AN UNHAPPY CHILD

Though she was not an especially rebellious young child, Gina became increasingly demanding to the point that she eventually became rebellious. While she may have appreciated her parents' generous ways as a child, experience taught her that she could demand favors from her parents and usually succeed in receiving them.

The following qualities may emerge in a selfish child:

+ Fails to see life from others' point of view.
+ Uses emotions in a manipulative way to control others.
+ Receives only limited enjoyment out of life's experiences.
+ Constantly searches for ways to gain ultimate happiness.
+ Gives little back to those who are generous with her.
+ Fights rather than give in to simple requests from others.
+ Misinterprets the motives of those who refuse to cater to her whims.
+ Fails to trust others, even though others are dependable.
+ Attempts to force opinions on others.
+ Fails to accept responsibility for poor judgment.

The selfish child builds an identity of herself that is based on the things she has accumulated, favors she receives, or privileges extended to her. A self-centered quality develops that prevents her from considering the needs of family members or friends.

When a child is young, it is natural and normal for her to expect to be given a lot from the adults in her world. Her limited skills in dealing with the world keep her from being able to meet her own needs satisfactorily. As the child grows, one of her needs is to learn to expand her world to include the needs of others. By the time a child reaches school age, she should be capable of extending herself to others by sharing, taking turns, or allowing others to have their way.

Gina's mother explained, "I felt we were doing a pretty good job of teaching Gina to share. I told her 'no' when she wanted to do something that was outrageous. But, if she wanted to do something and I saw no real harm in letting her do it, I simply gave in. Or, if she wanted me to buy her something and I could afford it, I bought it. I always told her she should appreciate what I did for her. I know I certainly would have appreciated it if my mother did for me the things I have done for her. When she was young, I thought she was thankful. Maybe she wasn't."

Reoccurring behavior patterns have a way of becoming habits. In the same way, expectations that are repeatedly met have a way of turning into demands. Gina learned that it was her mother's habit to try to meet all her wishes. Not wanting her mother to stray from this pattern of giving, Gina discovered that she could keep pressure on her mother to give beyond her need. Years of experience taught Gina that her mother had a hard time saying no to most requests. Mother's attempts to correct her earlier mistake of leniency could be swatted aside by childish emotional outbursts.

## CONTENTMENT IS JUST OUT OF REACH
A child who has been given more than she needs learns that satisfaction is never really reached. In actuality, the selfish child remains forever unhappy because she is chasing the wrong dream. Instead of finding happiness in relationships and accomplishments, this person looks for satisfaction in the form of power over others.

As I got to know Gina, I found I could talk openly and even bluntly to her about her preoccupation with herself. I explained to her, "When you were two years old, it was natural that you would want to overpower your mother and others by taking all you could from them. That's a natural thing for a two-year-old to do. At that time in your life, you were not able to understand that it was in your best interest to have limits placed around you.

"When you were very young, you had too much success getting others to give in to your wishes. Your mother felt you were appreciative, but actually you took advantage of your mother's kind heart." I smiled at Gina. She agreed with me and gave a sheepish grin back to me.

I explained Gina's dilemma to her: "Right now you're feeling a lot of unhappiness because you've come to expect too much from others. You know you need to give up some of the demands you put on your mother and even on your friends, but that also means giving up power you've gained over the years."

Again Gina grinned at my words. She knew I had hit her where it hurts—in her pride. She clarified what I had just told her: "Basically, you're telling me I have to accept it when my mother tells me I can't do what I want."

I verbally nudged her a little further in her thought: "Don't forget, I'm also saying you'll be happier if you let your mother make more of the decisions you've been making for yourself."

"Are you sure?" Gina wanted to feel the inner joy that she could only pretend to have, but wanted to make sure that letting go of her self-centered nature was the right thing. I nodded in response to Gina's question and said little more as Gina mulled over what we had discussed.

### ❖ THE GIFT OF SATISFACTION ❖

In our affluent society, I have seen many children who may be described as selfish in one way or another. The present generation of parents has not experienced material hardship in comparison to other previous generations of adults. As a result, more parents today are willing and able to give more to their children than they were given in their youth. The motives for parents' giving vary, but in most cases, because they want a better life for their child, parents give possessions and privileges that were not extended to them in their own childhood. Parents give partly to make up for what they did not receive.

As it becomes evident that a child is ungrateful for his parents' sacrificial efforts, it is common for parents to scramble for a discipline technique that will correct their child's behavior. Adults may try any of the following methods of attempting to instill thankfulness in a self-centered child:

- ◆ Reasoning with the child about the need to be more giving to others.
- ◆ Shaming him for selfish desires.

- Grounding the child until he agrees to share with a willing attitude.
- Bargaining with him in hopes that he will appreciate the parents' willingness to meet him halfway.
- Arguing with the young person because he will not accept the need for discipline.

I find that children and teenagers are aware of their parents' inability to find the best punishment to teach sharing. Gina told me, "When my parents punished me for being rude or selfish, I just tried harder to make them feel guilty. I knew if I could hurt them the way they hurt me, they probably would give in."

Gina's statement can teach us a lot about the way young people closely watch the motives of their parents. She was fully aware that her mother gave to her because she wanted to meet a need that had gone unmet in her own childhood. When her mother tried to teach Gina the need to be less demanding, Gina reacted by drawing out the guilt in her mother. Through her aggressive behavior, she sent a reminder to her mother: "Think back on your own childhood and remember how unhappy you felt when your mother didn't give you what you wanted. You don't want to see me go through the same pain you experienced, do you?"

❖     ❖     ❖

The Bible clearly teaches us to be giving people. Christ instructs His disciples, "Freely you have received, freely give."[1] Happiness has a cyclical nature. As we give to others in the form of service, consideration, kindness, or generosity, the same emotion returns to the giver. The cycle of happiness is broken when selfish desires prevent us from giving to others. A child who has been given too much fails to learn the joy of giving.

A task of parenthood is to share opportunities for happiness with our child. As we teach the young person to accept graciously what is given and give willingly as he is able, he will find satisfaction in life. The emotion of happiness cannot be forced on a child simply through discipline. It must be taught through the example of the adult leaders in the home.

Gina's parents learned to put limits around their daughter's excessive desires. That single correction helped teach her to be more content with what she had. They went beyond this adjustment and took a thorough inventory of their lifestyle and the lessons Gina learned by observing them. They discovered that by being more content with their own blessings, the need to satisfy Gina with temporary and artificial happiness lost its urgency.

In a home in which satisfaction outweighs selfishness, the following qualities are often displayed:

- Material gains are sought in moderation.
- Money and service is offered to those who are without.
- Time is made for relationships over accomplishments.
- Family needs are considered before personal desires.
- Complimentary remarks outweigh critical ones.
- Rewards are offered for generous actions.
- Emphasis is given to cooperation rather than competition.
- Personal strengths are accepted in a modest fashion.

The humility that accompanies happiness is taught through the discipline of training a child to accept all that is given with thanks. Parents who display personal satisfaction lead the child to follow, rounding out a family plan for contentment.

As Christ speaks of giving freely of the good that has been shown to us, He offers an important lesson in a few short words. The blessings of life are not to be hoarded and enjoyed in isolation. A blessing is not a blessing unless it is shared with others.

Gina learned that by collecting as many privileges and possessions as she possibly could, she could not find happiness. Only as she let go of her need to control what she accumulated from her family and friends did she experience real satisfaction. That lesson became clearer to her as her mother and father joined with her in building happiness in their family.

# ❖15❖

# *Exchanging Frustration for Gratitude*

**H**ank reluctantly handed a note to his mother as he arrived home from school. It was from his teacher, Ms. Bruner. The note read: "Mrs. Kaufman, I have some concerns about Hank I would like to discuss with you. Please contact me to arrange a conference." As Mrs. Kaufman read the note, she looked at Hank and asked, "Do you know anything about this?" Hank simply shrugged his shoulders, wanting to avoid any discussion about his school behavior.

During the conference, Mrs. Kaufman listened as Ms. Bruner explained her concerns: "I'm worried about how easily Hank gets upset when things do not go his way. He gets mad so quickly, it's hard for me to know how to handle him."

Mrs. Kaufman felt a bit defensive, but fully appreciated Ms. Bruner's concern. "I know he's not the easiest kid in the world to handle. What's he doing that gets him into trouble?"

"If he has a hard time on an assignment, he doesn't ask me for help. He simply gets mad and refuses to do the work. When I try to help him, he says he doesn't need my help. He shows a similar attitude toward the other students, too. If things don't go his way, he's likely to throw a fit and accuse the other children of treating him unfairly."

Mrs. Kaufman knew exactly what Ms. Bruner meant. Hank acted much the same at home. With exasperation, she explained to the concerned teacher, "Hank does all of those things at home, too. I honestly don't know what to do with him. If I discipline him, he just gets mad. If I ignore him, his behavior gets worse. Even when I'm nice to him, often he won't accept that. I don't know what to try next."

Teacher and parent both sympathized with the other. Neither could instill cooperation in Hank. Ms. Bruner offered a few suggestions to Mrs. Kaufman in hopes that they could work together to improve Hank's attitude. The mother listened carefully, but left the conference without the confidence that any of the suggestions would prove to be effective.

❖   ❖   ❖

Hank was a frustrated boy whose emotions actually mirrored those of each of his parents. As I talked with both parents in my office, Mrs. Kaufman explained, "I can hardly blame Hank for the way he acts in school. Kenneth and I are as frustrated as he is. Kenneth is a good husband, but things just never have gone the right way for our family."

Mr. Kaufman sadly shook his head and agreed with his wife: "I've had one long string of bad jobs. Every time I think I've come upon a good job, something goes wrong. I get laid off, my boss and I don't get along, or something else happens to make things go bad." Mr. Kaufman was an intelligent man, but could not find fulfillment in his work. In the twelve years of his married life, he had not worked longer than twelve months at any one job.

As Mr. and Mrs. Kaufman explained more about their home life to me, I began to understand its effect on Hank's behavior. Mrs. Kaufman stated, "Since Kenneth has never been satisfied in his work, he is in a foul mood most of the time when he is home."

I reacted to her comment: "It's probably easy for you to become upset, too, since your family life is not settled."

Mrs. Kaufman sighed heavily. "I can't tell you how overwhelmed both Kenneth and I feel. We got married when we were too young. We really had no business getting married at the time, but we both wanted to get out of bad home situations. My father left my mother when I was young, and I grew up under a lot of hardships. I never had anything that I wanted as a child. I became pretty rebellious. I wanted *and* needed to get out of my mother's house.

"Kenneth's situation was different than mine, though it wasn't any better. His dad almost forced him to rebel." Mrs. Kaufman looked at her husband, who silently agreed. She went on with her comments. "I don't think Kenneth likes to admit it, but his self-esteem is pretty low. He's got all kinds of ability, but he has no faith in himself. I think that's part of the reason he hasn't found his niche in life."

"Neither of you has recovered from a difficult childhood," I reacted. "I suspect that when you got married you thought life would get better right away, but it hasn't."

Both adults nodded as Kenneth verbalized his thoughts: "You're right. Things haven't gotten better. Sometimes I wonder where it's all going to end. I think I can handle my own frustration, but it hurts me to see our frustration show up in our son."

## FRUSTRATION CAN BE TAUGHT

Parents don't intend to teach a child to react negatively to the stress that is sure to confront him. Learning takes place as a child imitates the behavior of adults. While not all childhood behaviors are taught in this way, many of a child's emotional expressions are shaped by what is modeled at home.

Before a child actually imitates the behavior of his parents, he must first identify with their characteristics. In Hank's case, the frustrations of his school situation differed from the frustrations of his parents. But, he could easily identify with them as he heard any of the following statements:

- "My boss doesn't appreciate the work I do."
- "I feel like I'm going absolutely nowhere in life."
- "Nobody understands what it is like to feel the way I do."
- "If I could only get the right break, life would quickly get better."
- "I know what I'm capable of doing, but other people keep holding me back."

- "Life's not fair. I think I'm just about ready to give up."
- "If other people won't cooperate with me, I'm certainly not going to cooperate with them."

As a child observes his parents, he identifies those attitudes, thoughts, and emotions that give meaning to the adults' behavior. As these messages are expressed over and over, the child begins to see life in the same way. That is, he takes on qualities that define his mother or father (or both).

As a child identifies with his parents, it becomes easy for him to display their characteristics at school, in social settings, or even toward other family members. The child's identification with his parents influences his thinking. Once a child identifies with the thinking of his parents, the next step is similar behaviors.

Although a child will display different behaviors than an adult, there is often a remarkable parallel between the actions of a child and his parents. Note how Hank's behavior closely resembled the behavior of his parents:

| PARENTS' BEHAVIOR | CHILD'S BEHAVIOR |
|---|---|
| ◆ Complain that employers are unfair. | ◆ Gripes that teacher expects too much of him. |
| ◆ Critical and punitive toward children. | ◆ Acts aggressive toward peers. |
| ◆ Complain and sulk when upset. | ◆ Whines and cries when upset. |
| ◆ Attempt to overpower child by force. | ◆ Throws tantrums in attempts to control parents. |
| ◆ Blame spouse or child for conflict. | ◆ Blames parents for problems. |
| ◆ Fail to fulfill personal potential. | ◆ Makes poor grades in school. |
| ◆ Show anger through chronic depression. | ◆ Shows anger through disruptive behavior. |

Hank's behavior at school signaled a need for change in the way frustration was handled at home. As I talked with Mr. and Mrs. Kaufman, they recognized that Hank's need was not simply for stronger discipline; he also needed to see a change in the atmosphere at home. As they were able to redirect their own frustration into opportunities for personal growth, Hank was able to accept their leadership and identify with the new hope they had discovered.

## MISHANDLED STRESS

A child who expresses chronic frustration may be communicating his inability to manage the stresses of life. His misbehavior may be his way of saying: "The expectations you have of me are too heavy for me to carry." A child who also has frustrated parents as role models will bear the additional burden of having no one to turn to for help in dealing with life's strains.

Through his misbehavior at school, Hank sent a number of messages to his parents, including:

- I'm not happy because I feel so misunderstood.
- I want someone to step in and relieve the pressure I feel.
- I want to know that I will receive some successes in life.
- It's not fair that other kids have an easier life than I have.
- I need to find some way to fit in with others.
- I want some respect for the effort I have shown.

Mr. Kaufman remarked to me, "When Hank comes home from school with a bad report from his teacher, my tendency is to tell him, 'Hey kid, get used to it. Life doesn't get any better than what you see right now.'"

A frustrated child who lives with equally frustrated adults quickly comes to the conclusion that relief from emotional discomfort is nowhere to be found. That hopeless outlook only compounds his despair and leads to further feelings of defeat. He comes to believe that there is no way to release his emotions properly. He believes his only alternative, then, is to show his frustration through misconduct. His faint hope is that someone will recognize the desperation in his words and behavior and miraculously sooth his emotional pain.

## THE REWARDS OF FRUSTRATION

A child picks up new habits as a result of the responses given to his actions. Parents often set out to reward specific behaviors with the hope that good conduct will become a habit in the child. Yet, a child's negative behaviors are unintentionally rewarded. A child who acts out his frustrations through misbehavior will accumulate an odd assortment of prizes for his actions.

Note the following scenarios involving Hank and his parents that resulted in a "reward" for the young person:

> **SITUATION:** Feeling that nothing ever went his way, Hank threw temper tantrums to express his deep-felt emotions. Following his tantrums, his mother's tendency was to strike a deal with him to prevent further outbursts.
> **REWARD:** Temper outbursts resulted in diminished demands.

> **SITUATION:** Hank's father tried to explain the realities of life to Hank by stating, "You better quit complaining about everything, because you'll never get any sympathy from me." Hank responded with his own harsh remark, saying, "Well, then, I'm just going to quit trying!" Hank's comment drew a look of disgust from his father.
> **REWARD:** Hank took comfort in knowing that his father felt just as fed up with the situation as he did.

> **SITUATION:** Feeling isolated and lonely with his emotions, Hank cried and whined all evening about how hard school was for him. His parents spent a lot of their energy that evening criticizing Hank for acting so immature. Much of what they did that evening revolved around Hank and his constant complaints.
> **REWARD:** Hank got a lot of attention, albeit negative, from his parents.

A child like Hank needs positive attention, not the negative attention he thrusts on himself. The child's need to be rewarded is valid, but must be met in a constructive way, not in a way that promotes further frustration. The role of the parents is to recognize the hidden way the child may express his needs. When parents set aside personal feelings of frustration momentarily so the child's need can be met, it breaks the cycle of emotional pain and keeps it from repeating itself.

## ❖ THE GIFT OF GRATITUDE ❖

In the Bible, Paul expressed the same frustration each of us has experienced. He spoke plainly of the tug of war that went on within him personally. This is something even the most well-intentioned adult can identify with. In a completely honest emotional expression, Paul admitted, "I do not understand what I do. For what I want to do I do not do, but what I hate I do."[1]

Parents commonly say, "I don't know why I reacted to my child the way I did. I knew in advance that I was about to do harm to him, but I did it anyway." These words echo the feelings Paul expressed. I dare say there has not been a parent who has avoided feeling disgust for the way a family crisis was handled. The good news is that in the same way Paul used his personal frustration to learn how he could draw on the substantial strength of God, each parent can do the same.

Paul realized that if he ever reached a point of self-satisfaction, he would become spiritually stagnant. He had learned that by joining with the strength of God the heavenly Father, he could erase the failures of the past and move ahead, certain that his future would bring new opportunities for personal growth.[2] His frustration became a springboard for the kind of understanding that made him more effective in his service to others.

In his last known letter, an older and wiser Paul told Timothy, his adopted son, "What you heard from me, keep as the pattern of sound teaching."[3] Paul used his loving parental relationship with the younger Timothy as an opportunity to teach sound biblical guidelines for living. He knew that if he taught Timothy only rules for behavior, but did not also teach him through a loving relationship, Timothy would not climb out from under his own frustration as he met the inescapable hardships of life.

The life of Paul, as seen in the Bible, shows his progression from a disillusioned, frustrated young person to a content and influential adult. He took the frustrations of his own life as an opportunity to learn and teach others biblical truths. The conflicts of the past do not have to result in lasting disappointment. Past difficulties can pave the way for future family growth.

# ❖16❖

# *Exchanging Withdrawal for Relationship*

P hil expressed his feelings of rejection by his parents: "Everything I do around them seems to be the wrong thing. My dad
says I can't do anything right, and my mom is constantly
worried about how I'll make her look in front of her friends."

"So what do you do since you don't feel you can please your parents?" I asked Phil, hoping to gain insight into the motives of his
behavior.

The young person laughed as he told me, "I just go ahead and
do what I want to do and let them get mad. If they ask me why I did
that, I just keep it to myself."

I wanted to know more of Phil's thoughts. "You mean, you make
your parents guess about why you're acting the way you do?"

Phil became more serious and leaned forward as he talked. "Do
you know that my parents have no idea how depressed I am most of
the time? They think I'm just a brat, but they don't know how bad
I'm hurting inside."

"And the reason they don't know is because you won't tell them?"

"Why should I tell them? If I do, they'll just get upset. My dad
will ground me, and my mother will cry. I'm not going to tell them

anything I don't have to." Phil's exasperation showed as he spoke. He obviously wanted me to know the full impact of his pain.

I continued to try to understand Phil's point of view. "Tell me, Phil, does all this have a lot to do with your moody behavior? People describe you as a moody person. They never know what to expect from you."

Phil knew exactly what kind of information I wanted from him. "How would you feel if you always had someone breathing down your neck, criticizing everything you do? My dad is really hard on me. You'd keep things to yourself, too, if you got punished the way I do."

❖   ❖   ❖

Phil was brought to my office because he complained to his father that he "couldn't take it" any longer and wanted to get some help before he exploded emotionally. Though he was only fourteen years old, he knew his emotions were bottled up inside to a harmful degree. He scared himself one evening when he threatened to kill himself following a particularly bad argument he and his father had over a trivial matter. Feeling a need to make sense out of his emotions, he wanted to talk with someone outside his family.

As I counseled Phil and his family, I discovered that his behavior was a repetition of a cycle of unhappy family relationships. Phil was especially concerned about the pressure his dad placed on him to be "perfect." Phil explained, "My dad wants me never to make a mistake. If I do, he yells at me and tells me to do better. Then he grounds me. How can I prove anything when I'm grounded all the time?"

Phil's father, Foster, gave a different view of his intentions. Recalling his own childhood, he told me, "I know Phil thinks I'm rough on him. I wish he could fully appreciate what I had to go through when I was his age. He thinks he has it bad, but my dad expected ten times more from me when I was fourteen. I would have never dreamed of acting the way Phil does. If I had, my dad would have put me in my place real quick."

## MISUNDERSTOOD PARENTAL MOTIVES MAY PROMPT WITHDRAWAL

As I got to know Foster better, I realized that his intentions with his son were positive. He was hard on the boy because he wanted Phil to be self-motivated. He did not want his son to have to rely on anyone other than himself to be a success in life. He was hard on Phil in these ways:

- Mistakes were pointed out immediately so they could be corrected right away.
- "Bragging" about Phil was withheld so the youth would not become too content with his present accomplishments.
- Punishment was intentionally harsh so Phil would see the stark realities of life.
- Emotions were ignored because too much emphasis on emotions could make Phil vulnerable to people who were overpowering.
- Standards were set high in order to lift Phil's expectations of himself.
- Decisions were made for Phil so there would be no chance for him to be irresponsible.

Foster's desires for Phil were all positive. He wanted Phil to be:

- Well-rounded (aware of his strengths and weaknesses)
- Modest (graceful in accepting success)
- Realistic (mindful of the potential pitfalls of life)
- Decisive (capable of making difficult decisions)
- Goal-oriented (able to take care of his personal needs)
- Dependable (a person whose word was "gospel")

I explained to Foster that I could find no fault in the desires he had for his son. It is right and good for a parent to want a child to live up to his potential so he can make a valuable contribution to his world. Phil's behavior, however, suggested that he was not aware of his father's positive parental intent. The boy's poor communication style indicated that he felt misunderstood. Until Phil felt he was understood by his father, he was not likely to embrace his dad's goals as his own.

Foster was interested in making the changes needed to have a more helpful impact on Phil. He admitted, "I know Phil thinks I must hate him. I'm hard on him, but I'm doing it because I think he needs my help." As soon as Foster made that statement, he caught himself. "You know, Lee, it just dawned on me that my dad was certain that being hard on me was what I needed. I never did think he understood me. To this day we don't have a close relationship."

Foster was actually able to find humor in the similarity between his past relationship with his father and his present relationship with his son. "I'll bet my dad looks at me and thinks, *Look what a great job I did parenting Foster. He's successful in his work, lives in a nice home, has a wonderful wife and kids.* I'll bet he takes a lot of credit for where I am today." Foster chuckled as he recognized the irony of that thought.

"In a sense, your father did groom the qualities that make you successful by certain standards, but you seem to be aware of a few areas he neglected and their effect on your relationship with your own son." I hoped Foster could gain some understanding from his discovery of the reasons for much of his son's discomfort.

"My father was only concerned that I be a success in the status I achieved as an adult."

I added, "But he neglected to teach the value of relationships." Foster nodded in agreement.

❖   ❖   ❖

A withdrawn child frequently feels his need for healthy relationships has been ignored. A parent can discipline a child with the best of intentions, but if that discipline is offered outside the context of a strong parent-child bond, it is likely to misfire. Feeling that a part of his emotional needs have been ignored, the relationship-starved child is likely to become emotionally cold. The parent's desire to provide structure can lose its effectiveness because of the lack of an emotional connection between parent and child.

## WITHDRAWAL MAY SEEM LIKE SECURITY
Phil told me in our very first session, "I don't like to feel the way I do. I want to be happier." He could not understand the reason for his moodiness. I explained to Phil that there was a reason he acted the way he did. He quickly said, "I act like I do because I'm afraid of what's going to happen to me!"

Fear has a way of motivating a child to act in desperate ways.

Hoping to fight off the harmful effects of his fright, a child may resort to any of the following actions:

- Blaming others in the hope of placing the spotlight on someone else.
- Telling a lie in order to buy a little time to figure out what to do.
- Verbally striking out at others as a way of getting in the first blow.
- Clamming up to keep others from discovering ways they can do further damage.
- Making promises, without the intent to keep them, just to get a moment's relief.
- Gossiping about others to make personal faults seem small in comparison.
- Making ridiculous threats to intimidate others into backing down.
- Procrastinating in keeping responsibilities so others will compromise their demands.

A child is not completely defenseless against an overpowering adult. Although emotional withdrawal is not always a healthy alternative, the young person may feel it is his only alternative. A downtrodden child may have assumed that to be open and honest with others is likely to result in too much discomfort. Not wanting to walk into certain defeat, he may choose to keep his emotions to himself. In a child's way of thinking, the burden of heavy emotions is not as heavy as the weight of pressure from an overpowering adult.

## WITHDRAWAL MAY SIGNAL SENSITIVITY

Phil told me a number of times that one primary reason he refused to talk about his emotions was that he felt personally offended each time either of his parents reacted to him. All children are sensitive, but some are much more tender than others. Tender feelings can be both a strength and a weakness, depending on how they are expressed. Phil told me, "I get mad at myself when I get upset and cry, but I just can't help it. I try not to, but it just comes out."

Knowing that Phil was blaming himself for feeling out of control with his emotions, I responded, "Somehow it doesn't seem right to you that you should feel so upset. You think you should control your emotions better than you do, but it's hard."

Phil nodded, indicating those were his thoughts. He went on to tell me how he wished he was not as sensitive to his father's criticism and his mother's concern. "My mom tells me it's all right to cry, but my dad says I'm too old for that. It makes me feel dumb."

As I talked with Phil's parents about their son's need, I explained, "Phil's withdrawal from you is actually his way of telling you he wants to talk more openly to you." You can imagine the confused reaction I received from these adults.

Foster was interested in what I had said, but wanted further clarification. "How can that be? It seems that his refusal to tell us what he thinks is his way of saying just the opposite—that he *doesn't* want to talk."

"That's what it seems, but let's look at matters from Phil's point of view. At times he reveals at least some emotion. I think when he expresses his emotions, he is hoping to get a favorable reaction. If he gets that response, he talks more . . ."

". . . But if he doesn't, he clams up really fast." Foster completed my thought.

A child who is silent when he has emotions he should talk about may be sending a number of nonverbal messages, including:

- Everybody is against me. I'm all alone with my thoughts.
- I know you will disagree with me, so I'm not going to tell you what I think.
- I must not be an important person. If I was, you would listen to what I have to say.
- Other people seem so much more sure of themselves than I am.
- Nothing ever goes my way. Why should I bother to work to make things better?
- I'd give anything if I could talk openly to you and feel understood.

While a young person's verbal withdrawal may seem to be a sign that he is emotionally cold, his thoughts reveal he is sensitive and capable of being much warmer to others. Repeated episodes in which the young person leaves a conversation with much frustration can convince him it is in his best interest to just keep quiet—even if it hurts.

### ❖ THE GIFT OF RELATIONSHIP ❖

Christ reassured His worried disciples, stating, "Do not be afraid, little flock, for your Father has been pleased to give you the kingdom."[1] This tender expression can be that of a parent to his withdrawn child. I often find that children who withhold their emotions from their parents want very much to be assured that all is well. The intimidation the young person feels from the adult creates worry, which encourages him to keep his thoughts to himself.

The parent of the withdrawn child does not intentionally cause the young person to keep his emotions silent. Domineering is usually a form of protecting the child from possible harm. The entire family needs a balance to be struck between the child's uncertainty and the parent's force.

Whether they realize it or not, children are usually skilled at reading their parents' thoughts. Phil accurately told me, "My dad thinks he is helping me when he acts strict." That was his father's intent. But the boy's next statement told a lot about the actual effect of his father's protection. "I wish he would just loosen up. I can't talk to him when I know I'm going to get in trouble for telling him what I think."

At the root of Phil's withholding nature was a lack of a feeling of trust. He was not convinced that his father was sincere in his desire to protect Phil from emotional harm. He interpreted his father's strict ways as a lack of trust and overprotection from life's experiences.

A child begins to trust an adult when several communication conditions are met:

- When he is convinced his parent has listened fully to his point of view, a child is inclined to reveal his thoughts more fully.
- When the child hears her parent accurately paraphrase

her words to reflect her feelings, she can begin to understand herself more fully.

- As proper timing is used in making statements of constructive criticism, the child gains an appreciation for his
parent's courtesy toward him.
- The use of tact in making statements of constructive criticism encourages the child to be attentive.

As Foster and I worked together, he learned that he needed to
change his approach to protecting his son from emotional harm,
rather than his motive. He became more open with the young person
and less judgmental. Phil slowly reacted by showing greater honesty
in his emotional expressions.

Children need to know that their needs for protection are not
overlooked. Often we take so much care to watch over our children's
negative behaviors that we fail to meet their communication needs.
A child's desire to feel understood outweighs the need to give in to
an overpowering adult.

# ❖17❖

# *Exchanging Security for Independence*

**"I** can't do it!" wailed Carmen.

"What do you mean, you can't do it? Of course you can." Carmen's mother tried to reassure her doubting daughter. The girl was frustrated because she had to learn twenty new vocabulary words for a test in her language arts class on the following day. Obviously, Carmen did not agree with her mother as she continued to fret about her inability to learn so many words in such a short time.

The following day Carmen came home from school. With a dejected tone in her voice, she informed her mother, "We took that vocabulary test, and I didn't do too well."

Her mother stopped what she was doing and asked, "What did you score?"

"Sixty-eight," replied the girl as she looked away. "I told you I couldn't learn those words in just one night. I wish Mrs. Bell would give us more time to study before giving us a test. She's too strict."

Mother felt the need to offer her opinion. "I don't think Mrs. Bell is being strict. She just wants you to study hard. She wouldn't give you an assignment if she didn't think you could handle it."

As mother and daughter talked, the inevitable subject of Dad's coming reaction to her failing test score surfaced. Mom offered a suggestion: "Why don't you let me tell Dad about your grade? I think he'll take it better if I tell him. I can let him know that you didn't have much time to study." Carmen was more than happy to give that chore to her mother. She certainly did not want to be the bearer of bad tidings when her father arrived home later that day.

Dad did not take the news well. Even though his wife explained the difficulty of the assignment, he felt Carmen should have done much better. "How long does it take her to learn a few words? I'll bet she spent as much time worrying as she did studying. If she'd just put her mind to her studies, she wouldn't make such poor grades."

❖    ❖    ❖

Both Mr. and Mrs. Bradshaw were concerned about Carmen. Of their three children, she seemed to be the most fragile. She constantly complained that she could not do anything right. She seemed to have no confidence in herself. Each parent blamed the other for contributing to Carmen's timidity. Both adults saw her as being too dependent on them. She appeared to have no confidence in her abilities and always wanted others to do things for her.

## CRITICISM MOTIVATES SOME, CRUSHES OTHERS

Mr. Bradshaw made no excuses for his harsh ways. He admitted to being a tough dad and felt his method of parenting had its value. As a businessman, he expected as much from the people who worked for him as he did from his family. He firmly believed in demanding a lot, thinking people tended to live up to the expectations set before them. He was a workaholic and thought his children should accept his high standards as a model for their own performance.

Carmen was made from a different mold than her father. She caved in to his criticism of her and showed fear of his expectations rather than respect for his drive. She reacted to her father by:

- Avoiding him when she knew she had fallen short of his demands.
- Crying easily when asked to give an accounting of herself.

- Lacking confidence that she could gain his approval.
- Worrying about the response she might receive from him.
- Isolating herself when he was home.
- Accepting his punishment as confirmation of her lack of worth.
- Giving only half an effort on tasks for fear of rejection.

Mr. Bradshaw wanted to spur his daughter to take pride in herself. This was the design of his critical nature. He could not fathom her hesitance to try harder following a reprimand. He was puzzled that Carmen seemed to become increasingly inadequate as he tried to drive her to achieve.

The doubt that arises in the child from excessive criticism creates a greater dependence on others. Feeling unable to satisfy the demands of others adequately, a child may look to adults for answers because she has become convinced that she cannot find solutions to problems on her own. Parents then observe that the desired independent behavior takes a back seat to dependence on others.

## OVERPROTECTION CAN PRODUCE OVER-DEPENDENCE

Mrs. Bradshaw took a different approach to handling Carmen. She believed that by giving her daughter as much loving sympathy, understanding, and encouragement as she could, Carmen would respond favorably by accomplishing as much as she possibly could.

Mrs. Bradshaw told me, "I understand my daughter better than anyone else possibly could. I know exactly how she feels when her dad puts her down because he acts the same toward me. The difference is that I've learned to live with his ways. She just needs to do the same. I think she'll find that her dad's bark is worse than his bite."

Carmen was fully aware of her mother's protective manner. In a way she felt comfortable hiding behind the shield of her mother's concern. Yet she simultaneously felt unable to think for herself since she was convinced her mother would take responsibility for her. Carmen reacted to her mother's overprotective stance by:

- Letting her mother do things that she was capable of doing herself.

- Taking advantage of opportunities to make her mother feel guilty, knowing her mother would take responsibility for her.
- Whining that she could not do things with the hope that her mother would reduce the demands on her.
- Acting helpless in order to solicit words of encouragement from her mother.
- Turning away compliments with the complaint that she was not deserving of praise.
- Clinging to her mother when forced to face a new situation.

The wish of an overprotective parent is to keep the child from experiencing the hurt that could cause her to dig herself into an emotional shell. The irony of this way of relating is that the protected child sees her parent as security from life's difficulties rather than a source of strength. Instead of guarding the child from harm, the parent is preventing her from building the skills needed to fend for herself.

## CRITICISM AND OVERPROTECTION ARE SIMILAR

At first glance it would appear that the parenting styles of an overprotective parent and an overly critical parent have little in common. It is true that these two types of parents are quite opposite in their behaviors toward others. Yet, parents with these differing styles often have similar needs. The results of their interaction with a child may be remarkably similar.

I often find that both overprotective and overly critical parents have the same goals for their children, even though they are vastly different people. Some common desires of each adult include the wish to:

- Instill responsibility in the child.
- Provide a role model that the child can follow.
- Promote activities that will ultimately lead to success.
- Allow the child to make independent decisions.
- Recognize how the child can best use her strengths.
- Teach the child to think for herself.

- Motivate the child to take greater initiative in starting tasks.
- Teach the child how to get along with different types of people.

The overprotective parent hopes to achieve these goals by making life as free from stress as possible. This parent believes that the child will eventually come to appreciate the parent's efforts and respond by building independent work habits. Conversely, the critical parent believes the child will learn to face the demands of life by being forced to achieve.

The child is more likely to be confused by either method of parenting. She retreats from each adult by acting helpless. Rather than becoming independent, she comes to believe that she cannot do anything without outside aid. Each parent feels frustrated and often provides "more of the same" to convince the child to change.

The critical parent and the overprotective parent have similar beliefs about a child's capabilities, although these beliefs are shown through different behaviors. Here are some beliefs the overprotective and the critical parent may share:

- Unless I intervene, my child is not likely to fulfill her responsibilities.
- My child does not have the capacity for good judgment.
- It bothers me when my child makes errors.
- My child's lack of responsibility is a reflection on me.
- I'm afraid my child does not learn from his mistakes.
- My child needs to learn to control her emotions more effectively.
- It's up to me to teach my child to be independent.
- When given a choice, my child will probably make the wrong decision.

The beliefs parents have about a child often have a way of coming true. A child who receives the clear message that she is not capable will develop insecurities. She will not learn to function on her own for fear that she will not act according to her parents' wishes. To prevent herself from making errors in judgment, the child may take on a reserved stance. In her way of thinking, she won't make costly errors if she simply makes no decision at all. She defers most important decisions—and even those that are not so important—to others.

## DEPENDENCE PROMOTES SELF-DOUBT
The dependent child has difficulty viewing herself in a positive light. Self-image problems abound in this child. Carmen was convinced that she had few strengths but many weaknesses. She frequently compared herself to her friends and siblings for evidence of her inadequacies. She accepted her relative lack of social and academic success as proof that she could not live up to the expectations of her age group. The reactions she received from her parents confirmed her thoughts.

Children are like sponges when it comes to gathering beliefs about themselves. They absorb all the comments and reactions given to them by others. A child may learn that she receives a lot of attention when she acts helpless. At the same time, though, she may get little affirmation when she puts herself out on a limb to try new skills.

As time passes, the dependent child builds a set of beliefs about herself that only encourage further helplessness. These include:

- I should play it safe when I come upon a risky situation.
- Why should I extend myself to others since they are likely to reject me?
- If I let others help me, they can share the pain that will come when I fail.
- I feel lonely because no one else feels quite like I do.
- I don't really trust that others are interested in my welfare.
- I feel out of control when I do something on my own.
- I'll let others make decisions for me since they are more likely to be correct.
- If I do something right, it must have been a mistake.
- I have to admit that I usually expect the worst to happen to me.
- There's no way I can live up to everyone's expectations.

The negative thought pattern of the dependent child only makes matters worse for her. She sets herself up for repeated failures and her beliefs are reinforced by others' reactions. In a cyclical fashion, the adults encourage dependence in the child since it becomes increasingly evident that the child needs almost constant supervision.

Mrs. Bradshaw told me, "I feel I have to take over for Carmen. If I don't, I know exactly what will happen—she'll fall flat on her face."

Mr. Bradshaw expressed a similar thought: "If I don't ride that girl hard, she won't get anything done right. She has to have constant pressure put on her or she won't learn to get along in this world."

Both parents had the same belief about Carmen. They believed that their daughter could not behave independently. Carmen received their message loud and clear and lived up (or down) to their expectations. Her ineffective management of responsibilities kept the family in a spiraling pattern of defeat.

### ❖ THE GIFT OF INDEPENDENCE ❖

I will periodically ask parents what their objectives are as they lead their child through childhood and adolescence. Among the many responses I receive, I almost always hear parents say, "I want my child to become a happy and independent adult." I find it interesting that most adults connect happiness with independence. It is true that unless a child learns to view herself as a person capable of making wise decisions she will have difficulty finding happiness.

I believe the dependent child gives parents burdensome choices to make about what is in her best interest. That choice is made more difficult by the background experiences the adults may have had in their own childhood. Tenderhearted parents, like Mrs. Bradshaw, may believe that strictness and force have no place in the family because of their own fear of overpowering people. Critical parents, like Mr. Bradshaw, may have entered parenthood believing that a child should be taught to overpower others to avoid certain defeat. Both parents draw on their background of experiences in making choices about how to respond to a developing child.

A primary need of overly dependent children is a patient and encouraging home atmosphere. Few children actually enjoy being dependent on others; virtually all want to free themselves from the chains that bind them to others who are more powerful and often overbearing. Children often lack initiative because they do not know where to begin in their quest to change, not because of a lack of desire.

As we understand the duties of parents, we recognize that leadership responsibilities include setting the tone for a positive environment in the home. Parents should convey to the child a belief in her abilities to be independent. Encouragement and praise can replace criticism and worry. To decrease dependence on others and replace it with independence, the following guidelines are helpful:

- Give your child tasks she can easily perform. Comment favorably on her success.
- Offer your child choices. Let him make decisions about what he will do. Refrain from criticizing his choice.
- Avoid emotional exchanges in which your child is sent the message that she is inadequate.
- Make frequent use of phrases such as "That's something you can do."
- Rehearse problem-solving strategies with your child. Praise him for any improvement.
- Listen with interest when your child expresses her frustration, but avoid accepting her problem as your own.
- Get out of the trap of motivating your child by threat or punishment. Motivate positive behavior with rewards and encouragement.
- Refrain from making decisions based on your emotions. Be objective as you decide what is best for your child.

God has placed you in a position of leadership in the home. Your child is dependent on you for guidance throughout childhood. Many children will attempt to stay in a dependent posture since they have found a certain comfort in relying completely on others. You must keep your child from sacrificing temporary comfort at the expense of damaged feelings of self-worth. As dependent children learn that they are capable, they then can approach adulthood with the ability to assume responsibility for those who must depend on them. They can find happiness in independence.

CHAPTER

*18*

# Exchanging Control for Boundaries

**M**rs. Bailes received a phone call late at night. As she answered the phone, she immediately recognized the voice of the speaker. It was the father of her son's best friend. "Helen, I'm sorry to bother you so late at night, but I felt I had to let you know what Dan and Todd have gotten themselves into."

As Mrs. Bailes heard those words, her heart leapt into her throat. She just knew there would be awful news about her son. The kind of reckless lifestyle he was pursuing frightened her. She was constantly worried of something harmful happening to him. Todd was sixteen years old and felt no need to go by any authority's guidelines. Mrs. Bailes had given up trying to control him long ago. Her lone hope now was to try to contain him to prevent him from disaster. She could only hope that when Todd reached adulthood, he would voluntarily choose to slow down his fast-paced way of living in favor of one that was more settled.

"What's happened, Kenneth? Are the boys all right? What did they do?"

Kenneth tried to be calm as he spoke because he knew Mrs. Bailes would be alarmed by his call. "They're all right, Helen. They're here at my house. Todd knows I'm on the phone with you. They were just escorted here by the police. It seems they got caught riding through a neighborhood smashing mailboxes with a baseball bat. On top of that, they had been drinking and were making a pretty bad scene with some other boys who were chasing them until the police stopped the whole ordeal."

Mrs. Bailes felt sick to her stomach. By now her husband was awake and could tell that something was wrong. "What are we supposed to do? Are the police still at your house?"

"There's really nothing you can do right now. We'll let Todd sleep over here tonight. We can talk more in the morning, but I felt obligated to let you know what had happened. The police officer gave me his name and phone number. He's going to see to it that the boys are held responsible for what they've done."

Mrs. Bailes thanked Dan's father and hung up the phone. She explained the situation to her husband. He immediately became upset and made threats about how he would take care of Todd by punishing him severely. After a few minutes, the couple tried to rest and go back to sleep, but could not.

❖    ❖    ❖

I came to know Todd shortly after "the mailbox incident," as he called it. He was angry at having to come to my office. He felt it was enough to be punished for what he had done, but he didn't need to talk to a psychologist. I explained to Todd that I would like to study his family from his point of view to determine any changes that would help his family run more smoothly. Once I understood him, his family and I could talk together. He liked that idea and actually expressed hope that changes could be made. Of course, his plan was that the changes made would give him a free ride through the remainder of his teenage years.

## WHO'S IN CONTROL OF THE HOME?
When I counsel children and teenagers, I often find myself quickly asking the question: *Who is in control of the home?* The answer often provides an important key to unlocking doors of disharmony in a family. I believe that the God-ordained pattern of the family places parents at the helm in a position of leadership. Parents use a variety

of methods to exercise their leadership. These are the three most important elements that determine who is in control of the home:

- ◆ The emotional climate of the home.
- ◆ The style of discipline used to teach responsible behavior.
- ◆ The communication family members use with one another.

Even from a young age, a child will try to gain control over the family. The next time you are with a preschool-age child, watch how he tries to direct the traffic of the household. He will act in such a way that the entire family takes on his mood. He may try to offset the power adults can show through discipline by challenging his parents to one battle after another. Through both words and behavior, he will make his opinions clearly known.

While it is natural for a child to attempt to control the tempo of the house, the young person needs the leadership of his parents. Without it, the mistakes the young person might make could end in disaster. Yet, the behavior of the adults in the home may offer a child the opportunity to step in and take charge of the family.

❖      ❖      ❖

Todd smiled when I asked him to describe each of his parents for me. "Who do you want me to start with?" he asked, with the implication that he wanted the chance to lay out his charges against each parent.

"That's something you can decide."

Todd thought briefly and stated, "Then I'll begin with my dad. Dad can't stand how I get into trouble all the time. Every time he hears that I've gotten into trouble, he blows his top—big time!"

"You mean like when you got caught by the police smashing mailboxes?"

Todd smiled. "Yeah. He couldn't say too much about that, though. He knew I had been drinking, but if he tried to get me for that, he knew I'd throw it back in his face that he drinks all the time. When that subject comes up, he can't do anything but make excuses."

I wanted to know how Todd used his father's drinking as a weapon. "So you can take some pressure off yourself simply by putting pressure on your dad."

"Something like that, yeah. He yells for a while and says he's going to ground me, but I know he won't. If he did, I'd tell Mom about some of the things he does and then he'd be in the doghouse with her."

Todd's comments about his father told me a lot about who was in control of his family. This teen had learned through years of experience that he could hold his father hostage by making good on threats to harass him about his drinking problem. Although Dad attempted to overpower the youth through threats, punishment, and criticism, Todd had learned that a few well-placed words and well-timed actions could overrule his dad's authority.

## COMPETITION CAN DESTROY A FAMILY

Some words in our vocabulary have both a positive and a negative meaning, depending on how the word is used. The word *competition* can suggest the profitable give and take between individuals that encourages healthy exchanges to take place. Wholesome give and take can motivate family members to be all they can be for the good of the family.

Conversely, *competition* can be harmful when it produces a rivalry among family members that robs the family of its sense of unity. A family that sees too much competition will fight for individual causes, disrupting togetherness. Examples of how unhealthy competition can develop between parents and their children are as follows:

- ◆ A child feels neglected by his mother who works many hours outside the home. Whenever his father and mother do something special that does not include him, he misbehaves as a way of making them aware of his need for attention.

- ◆ A girl feels that her father always sides with her mother rather than looking at matters from her point of view. Tired of feeling left out, the girl throws a temper tantrum to demonstrate her outrage.

- ◆ A young boy believes he is punished too often by his parents. He would like a louder voice in the decisions that directly involve him. He complains loudly that nobody understands his needs.

♦ A teen thinks she is being forced to accept rules that are much stricter than is necessary. She shows her desire to take charge of her own life by flagrantly violating the parents' rules.

As I got to know Todd, we talked of his tendency to compete for control with his parents. He could not agree with their treatment of him. He accused his father of being a hypocrite. He said his mother was old fashioned. He felt he had some great ideas about what would work to give him a greater feeling of satisfaction. He thought he should be given complete exemption from rules and be allowed to make up his own mind about matters that influenced him.

Todd's parents knew they could not agree with their son's wishes. Their approach to handling this dilemma was to try to convince him, through lectures and punishment, that their understanding of his needs was superior to his. They were correct in assuming that Todd was too immature to make some of the decisions he wanted the freedom to make. They allowed him, however, to pull them into an unhealthy competition with him when they gave in to the urge to fight with him for control.

## KIDS LOOK FOR LOOPHOLES

A young person who is convinced that he does not need guidance from his parents will look for loopholes that allow him to slip through the boundaries that have been placed around him. Through experience, he has learned that he can change his parents' expectations of him in a variety of ways.

I made a comment in one of my sessions with Todd: "Your parents have a lot of rules for you to follow, and I think you would agree that most of the rules are pretty reasonable." I smiled at him as I continued, "Somehow, though, you have found a way around most of those rules. How do you do it?"

Todd smiled back at me as if he were about to reveal the secret of his success. "I know how to break the rules so that my parents have no choice but to give in to me."

I asked him if he would reveal some of the tricks he used to dominate his parents. He named several loopholes that allowed his behavior to go unaccounted:

- "My dad backs off when I bring up his habit of drinking."
- "If I can get my parents into an argument about me, one of them will take my side. Then, I can take advantage of the one who's more lenient."
- "If I can make my mom cry, she gives in, even if she's really mad at me."
- "When I hound my parents to lighten the punishment they've given me, most of the time they will, just so I'll leave them alone."
- "I'll accuse my dad of being worse to me than his dad was to him. He didn't like his dad, so it hurts him to hear me say that."
- "I promise that I won't do something again. My parents, especially my mother, really want to believe me. If I sound convincing enough, they'll usually compromise."

A young person usually has a greater understanding of his parents' emotional makeup than we assume. He knows where his parents' strengths are and also where their weaknesses are located. Naturally, as the child attempts to manipulate his parents, he will avoid his parents' strengths and prey on those weaknesses.

A child does not need to know the complete family history to be capable of taking advantage of circumstances from his parents' past that can give him an edge in controlling the family. Todd did not know the details of the relationship between his father and grandfather. He only needed to know that his dad did not want to experience the same type of conflict with his son that he had experienced years earlier with his own father.

Mr. Bailes told me that he recalled his father giving him awful beatings when he was young simply because he had violated a minor household rule. He grew up frightened of his father and had little affection for the man. During his adolescence he rebelled by breaking every rule he could just to make his father mad. Now that he had a son who displayed similar behavior, he felt both guilty and helpless.

He knew of no other way to teach proper behavior to his son than to try to force him into submission the same way his father had done.

All Todd needed to know was that his father felt helpless. He was not concerned with the details of how that feeling came about. He simply recognized a loophole and slipped through it. In the same way that he found weaknesses in his father's emotional armor, he also knew of shortcomings in his mother's character that gave him the opportunity to manipulate her.

Mrs. Bailes had also grown up under an abusive father. Not only did her father punish her with unnecessary physical force, he belittled her femininity by making frequent statements that were sexually loaded. She was frightened of her father and learned not to trust men. When she became a mother, she vowed to teach her son respect for others, especially females. Todd did not know precisely how his grandfather had damaged his mother. He simply knew that something about his mom made her vulnerable to his underhanded behavior. When she became upset over his behavior, he could pounce on her worries and get what he wanted from her.

Children are aware that parents come into adulthood with habits they picked up from their own family experiences. I often find that children are more perceptive of the parents' vulnerable qualities than the adults are. Not willing to show the kind of patience that grooms family relationships, the young person typically pushes ahead to take the position of control in the family.

### ❖ THE GIFT OF BOUNDARIES ❖

When we speak of the need for *control* in the family, it is important to understand how a child defines this term. Parents have a tendency to try to control the child's *behavior* by paying close attention to family rules, boundaries, punishments, and the like. Conversely, the child pays close attention to the *emotions* displayed by the parents. A child can take charge of a household when he realizes he can dictate the emotions of his family members. A powerful sense of superiority comes to a young person when he knows he is the one who determines whether the parents will be satisfied or angry.

Effective parental control of the household can be gained by following these guidelines:

◆ Dare to view the world as your child views it. Whether or not you agree with his position, it is very helpful to you to understand the reasoning behind his behavior.

◆ Refrain from attempting to change your child's feelings or opinions. When you try to reason with your child she will quickly frustrate you by refusing to accept your logic.

◆ Constantly remind yourself that your task is to provide leadership to your child, not to dictate how he will think or feel. As you detach yourself from your child's inner reactions, you will find increased ability to show gentleness, patience, and self-control.

◆ Focus only on the behavioral guidelines you have established rather than on your child's reaction. Follow through with what has been promised. Say no more than is necessary to implement the family rules. It is not necessary that your child voice agreement with you.

◆ At a later time, let your child voice any negative emotions. If she is in a receptive mood, briefly tell her your emotions. Choose to discuss emotions when the atmosphere is calm, not when it is potentially explosive.

To retrieve the rightful control from a power-hungry child, parents must be able to step outside their emotions and react with the kind of composure that sends a message: *I will decide the emotions I express.* Recall the oft-quoted charactistics that are evidence of having God's Spirit: "The fruit of the Spirit is love, joy, peace, patience, kindness, goodness, faithfulness, gentleness and self-control."[1]

I have to admit that I squirm as I read through that list of characteristics. It takes a lot of personal dedication and reliance on God to groom those qualities. I take comfort in knowing, though, that even Paul, who wrote those words, must have had difficulty with his own admonition to others. We know that his life was marked by numerous incidents in which he tried to force control on others inappropriately. We have to assume that through his devotion to a different way of life he came to be more objective about his reactions to others. Rather than forcing others to give in to his way of thinking, Paul led by example. He came to realize that his influence on others was much more positive when he was completely open to the personal changes he could make by opening himself to the full grace of God.

❖     ❖     ❖

Todd never did admit that he was willing to accept the boundaries his parents attempted to place around him. He continued to push the limits back as far as he could. But, as his parents let go of their need to force control on him, he came to realize that he could no longer take advantage of their emotions. The tide of authority in the family returned to the parents.

In our final session, Todd told me, "I still feel the way I've always felt. I guess my mom and dad do, too. We're not arguing as much, though, and that makes it easier to live in my home."

As I tried to read between the lines of Todd's statement, I believed he was saying he was willing to let go of some of the control he had seized from his parents. Even though he had relinquished some of the authority he had assumed over the family, there was a sense of relief that his family was not in a constant battle. He was willing to trade some of his power for peace in the home.

CHAPTER

## ❖19❖

# *Exchanging Conflict for Choices/Consequences*

Sitting across from me in my office were the distraught parents of a thirteen-year-old girl. They were uncomfortable at the thought of having to see a psychologist about their daughter. The husband, Ben, explained to me, "Kate and I have talked about our children numerous times, and we both agree that we never dreamed we would end up having trouble with Jennifer. When she was younger, she was the one we could always count on to do what we asked. She never gave us a moment's trouble until she entered the sixth grade. But since that time, the roof has fallen in. It's like we have a completely different child in our home."

When I first met Jennifer, I immediately understood the mixture of emotions her parents felt. She was immaculately dressed and spoke to me with evidently well-groomed social manners. At the same time, I could sense an air of haughtiness in her, which revealed that the sweetness that had been present years earlier had somehow vanished.

"I don't know what my parents told you about me, but it probably wasn't good, was it?" Jennifer inquired, to see exactly what my preconceived notions were about her.

"Your parents are concerned that things are not quite the same as they used to be at home. They're hoping they can be close to you once again." I was careful not to alienate her with an accusatory remark.

Jennifer rolled her eyes as she listened, then gave her response: "My parents want me to be a cute little girl like I used to be." With a snicker she added, "But there's no way I can ever go back to that again."

I wanted to know more of what this young girl thought. "How's that?" I asked.

"You see, when I was little, I did everything I was supposed to do. But I found out I can do things my way, without someone watching every little move I make. I learned that I can make up my own mind."

"You figured out that you're your own person," I responded, hoping to gain clarification of what Jennifer meant.

Jennifer began to sense that I was looking at life from her point of view. She nodded, "Yeah, I guess you could say that."

"When you were young, though, you didn't think for yourself. You let your mom and dad think for you. Is that right?" I wanted Jennifer to elaborate further on her ideas.

"It was more like my mom and dad forced me to think like they did. Like, I remember when I was young, I couldn't do anything unless my mom was right there with me. I used to cry when my mom would take me to school because I didn't want her to leave."

"But now it seems you can't get enough freedom from your parents."

"I'll say!"

"So that's where your parents see rebellion. You want more freedom, but you feel you have to force your feelings on them. It's like you're pushing everybody away from you."

Jennifer added, "And I'd like them to get as far away as they possibly can."

## COMPLIANCE MAY BE A DISGUISE

Some of the most difficult children to "read" correctly are often those who have a pattern of obedient behavior. I see many children who, as they reach their teenage years, seem suddenly to turn from angels to monsters without a reasonable explanation. When these young people are willing to share their thoughts openly, they will make a variety of statements to suggest they have wanted to let loose with their emotions for quite some time, but held tightly to them for fear of being misunderstood.

These are some thoughts of the suddenly rebellious child:

- I'm tired of being smothered by people who think they know what's best for me.
- I can't stand being thought of as a "good kid" when I don't feel like being good.
- Nobody knows the real me. Well, they're about to find out who I really am.
- So what if I offend someone? I'm only concerned about my feelings, not everybody else's.
- Now that I've vented my frustrations, I like the way it feels. I'm going to keep it up.
- If someone tries to tell me to go back to my old way of doing things, I'll tell them where they can get off!

Some children practically beg their parents to be in charge of their lives when they are young. Obliging parents may feel they are doing the right thing by attending to the needs of their child. As the child grows older and realizes she can exercise greater authority over her life than she thought, rebellion takes the place of compliance.

Jennifer's mother told me, "I feel betrayed by my own daughter. When Jennifer was younger, I would break my neck just to be there when she needed me, because she seemed to want me. Now I have a sassy teenager as thanks for the hard work I've put into being a mother."

## CHILDREN CAN BE PERCEPTIVE

As I study family patterns, I find that even preschool-age children are often aware of their parents' personal struggles. Although they cannot put words to their intuitions, they can quickly recognize an opportunity to take advantage of the parents' emotions.

Kate had a secret only a few people knew about. Other than her husband and a few close family members, no one else was aware that she had been sexually molested by her stepfather. This repeated experience of horror brought her into adulthood wearing many emotional scars. After she got out of her dreadful childhood environment and married, she vowed to put her past behind her and raise her children the way she wished she had been raised. She was convinced she had been a good mother, but wondered where she had gone wrong with Jennifer.

In a separate meeting, Jennifer told me of her recollections of her early relationship with her mother: "My mom has always been the type who worries about every little thing. Even when I was young she worried that something would go wrong when I was away from her."

Remembering that Jennifer had told me about her own reluctance to separate from her mother in her early years, I commented, "And when your mother worried about you, it was easy for you to cling to her for support. I wonder, were you giving your mother comfort, or did you want to be comforted?"

The teen thought for a moment, then responded, "Both. I think it was both."

"You mean that even when you were much younger, you knew how much your mother depended on you?"

"Yeah! She's always needed me worse than I needed her!" Jennifer did not know the source of her mother's need, but even in early childhood, she had been aware that something must have caused her mother to enter parenthood with a desire to make up for lost family fulfillment. Jennifer didn't have to know the details of her mother's history of abuse. She simply knew that her mother's anxious nature offered an opportunity to hide from her own need to be responsible to herself.

## GUARDING AGAINST HARMFUL SELF-CENTEREDNESS

Children come into the world with a receptive approach to life. They look to others to satisfy their needs since they are so helpless to provide for themselves. A task of parenthood is to provide for the needs of the child, while simultaneously teaching her to accept responsibility for her own needs as she is able. Parents have difficulty at times knowing when to break the emotional ties with a child and allow the child to fend for herself. This difficulty in knowing when to let go is the result of a lack of learning from past family relationships.

Kate entered parenthood without knowing what a healthy parent-child relationship should be. Her stepfather had been emotionally cruel, while her mother had been afraid to face the reality of the nightmare her child lived. Kate simply knew she had not been shown the kind of love that creates the feeling of worth she wanted to instill in her children.

When Jennifer was young, Kate relived her own childhood needs through her child. She smothered her child with the kind of affection she never received. She was concerned for her child's well-being. She took an active role in Jennifer's activities to prove her own position of importance in the family.

All of Kate's motherly plans were good. Yet, because of her history of family discord, she did not know when or how to break the bond with her daughter that would allow Jennifer to become an independent person. Through her rebellious behavior, Jennifer was, in essence, breaking that tie for her mother. Unfortunately, though, the teenager had become so accustomed to being catered to emotionally, she viewed the world in a self-centered way. She would not allow herself to extend herself to meet the needs of her family members.

A child with self-centered thoughts often has many of the following behavioral characteristics:

- ◆ Refuses to consider opinions other than his own.
- ◆ Tends to do what feels good at the moment without thinking of the future.
- ◆ Makes demands for freedom, but simultaneously rejects the idea of being held accountable for mistakes.
- ◆ Blames others for things that go wrong in the family.
- ◆ Rejects the reasoning and logic offered by adults who have experienced much more of life.
- ◆ Gets mad easily when others do not meet her demands, even if those demands are unreasonable.
- ◆ Fails to show gratitude for favors done by others.
- ◆ Overstates emotions in order to manipulate others.
- ◆ Feels easily offended when offered constructive criticism, regardless of its value.

Parents do not set out with the purpose of creating self-centered thoughts in their children. Jennifer, and others like her, do not hear the words, "Think of yourself and ignore the needs of others." Yet, a young person may take this stance because of a void in the life of a parent. The parent may attempt to provide for her child based on the needs that were ignored in her own childhood. In the process, the young person may get the wrong message about how she is to see herself in relation to others.

## ❖ THE GIFT OF CHOICES/CONSEQUENCES ❖

After a child has become difficult to manage, parents often have an overwhelming urge to convince her to change her ways. Usually, that desire takes the form of talking to the young person about why she needs to change. However accurate the parents may be, a child who is caught up in her own pattern of behavior will typically reject any guidance that is offered. The child may be so convinced that she is correct in the choices she makes, she cannot see the certain calamities that lie ahead.

Discipline is often used as a way of trying to instill in the rebellious child respect for the needs of others. But, along with the tendency to discipline comes tremendous parental frustration. No parent really enjoys having to correct a child constantly. The child reads her parents' frustration as an opportunity to manipulate, and does so, even if it means temporary discomfort.

❖    ❖    ❖

The Bible instructs us to refrain from the kind of excessive communication or force that causes another person to turn away from the lesson we would like to pass on. Instead, we often do our greatest teaching when we take action. We see evidence of this effective teaching method in the behavior of the Lord Jesus.

Consider Christ's encounter with a paralytic man, which is recorded in Mark's gospel. The man's friends had lowered him through the roof of a house in hopes that Jesus would heal him. Jesus did heal this man, and it created quite a stir among certain religious leaders who were looking for any reason to belittle and demean Christ's actions. Jesus had every reason to verbally thrash those who took issue with His concern for the man's needs. Instead, however, He allowed His actions to stand alone. He knew that to criticize would only diminish His potential influence over those who disagreed with Him, even though the words He could have chosen would have been valuable teaching tools.

This incident is only one example of how Christ refrained from the verbal banter and forceful behavior that would only encourage struggles between Himself and those with whom He wanted to have a relationship. Viewing Christ as our perfect example, we can take from His behavior a lesson in how we can effectively relate to family members who have grown increasingly difficult to deal with. *It is often wise to say less in the face of ongoing conflict.*

Kate and her husband, Ben, had an important question about their daughter: *What do we do to handle a rebellious child who used to be easy to live with?* Often the answer to such a question lies not in what we do, but in what we *refrain from doing.* Jennifer's parents, especially her mother, had reacted to this young person out of their own need. They had tried to force a kind of happiness in their daughter that Kate had not known when she was young. By becoming so heavily invested in the life of this child, they prevented her from coming to her own conclusions about how she could get along with others effectively.

When a parent tries to compensate for the past through the life of a child, that history may have a damaging effect on the child's life in the present. To have a positive effect, the child needs to know that life is seen from her point of view rather than as a continuation of the parent's past.

Kate and Ben learned that providing for Jennifer's needs did not involve shielding her from all of life's negative experiences. They found that by placing limits around their daughter, whether or not she agreed, she could come to her own understanding about how she should behave. Giving Jennifer the chance to voice her opinions openly encouraged her to think more deeply about the effect her choices could have on others. Jennifer found that it was not necessary to manipulate others to get her way in life. She became more open to others' needs in addition to her own.

# PART

# 4

# LEAVING THE PAST BEHIND— QUALITIES OF THE MATURING PARENT

❖

"I don't understand why the Bible tells us to be perfect in the same way that God is perfect. That's impossible!" The mother who made that statement intended to be the kind of parent she felt her child needed. She constantly read and studied the Bible to find ways she could improve her relationships with her husband and two young children.

One sentence really bothered this mom. In the famous Sermon on the Mount, Jesus said, "Be perfect, therefore, as your heavenly Father is perfect."[1] Theologians and other students of the Bible have long studied this teaching of Christ. It is generally agreed that, by encouraging perfection, Christ is stimulating His followers to be in a constant state of emotional and spiritual growth.

Jesus' words parallel those God the Father spoke to Moses: "Be holy because I, the LORD your God, am holy."[2] This guideline is followed by many other words of instruction, telling how a person should be set apart from the ordinary in the same way God is set apart from all humankind. Achieving wholeness involves making many small adjustments, not just one huge and instant change.

As I counsel parents and young people, I talk of how each of us needs to know his or her own personal strengths and weaknesses in a thorough way. After we have been totally honest with ourselves, we become capable of making the kind of permanent changes that push us toward that goal of maturing into the person God intended us to be.

In the previous pages, we have looked at the ways a parent's past may affect his own behavior and the behavior of his child. We will now take a more active look at how more mature parental qualities can have a tremendously positive impact on a family's life. While it may seem that developing the characteristics described in the following pages represents an awfully tall mountain to climb, I encourage you to put on your emotional hiking boots and begin the trek.

When we look at the lives of Bible characters who went through a transformation, we quickly see that God takes us right where we are and guides us through the maturation process. Our responsibility is to take the needed steps toward growth, one at a time. As we succeed in making small improvements in our way of relating to our children, we will eventually look back and find that we have come a long way toward family fulfillment.

CHAPTER

## ❖20❖

# *Listening*

**N**ine-year-old Nelson walked in the back door of his home, calling, "Mom! Where are you? Mom!"

Hearing her son, Mrs. Pendleton responded, "I'm right here, Nelson."

Nelson launched into a long story of how he had been treated unfairly by the boys next door. They were playing a modified version of "Saturday Night Wrestling," and Nelson was "body slammed" by one of the older boys who envisioned himself as the neighborhood wrestling champ.

Mrs. Pendleton took a seat at the nearby kitchen table and listened as Nelson gave a blow by blow description of his mistreatment. Once the child had finished his story, he waited expectantly for his mother to offer her solution to his predicament. Feeling no need to solve Nelson's problems for him, she said, "It hurts in a lot of different ways to be treated the way Luther just treated you."

Nelson was not satisfied with his mother's passive reaction. "Yeah, it hurts! And I'm going to hurt Luther the same way he hurt me!"

Mrs. Pendleton looked at her son with a feeling of concern. She

163

knew he felt hurt both physically and emotionally. After a brief moment, she said, "I'd bet that it hurts even more to think that maybe Luther hurt you on purpose."

With that statement, Nelson's eyes began to water slightly. He quietly acknowledged, "Yeah, it does." The bruised child went to his mother and accepted the hug she offered him. After a moment of silence, Nelson pulled away.

"Where are you headed?" asked the patient adult.

"I'm going upstairs. I want to call Jeff to see if he'd like to come over and play a video game with me."

Later that evening, Mrs. Pendleton went into the living room to relax for a few minutes before it was time for the children to get ready for bed. Placed in her customary chair was a note. Unfolding it, she looked at a drawing of a boy and his mother standing next to each other holding hands. Below the figure of the boy was written "Nelson" and below the adult was written "Mother." In the child's handwriting was a brief note that said, "I love you, Mom."

Mrs. Pendleton did not need to ask Nelson what inspired him to give her a handmade expression of affection. She knew he was saying, "Thanks for understanding me earlier this afternoon." Standing nearby, Nelson was watching his mother's facial expression as she read his note. Motioning for him to come to her, she thanked the boy with another big hug and a kiss.

IT FEELS GOOD TO BE UNDERSTOOD

Probably the most common complaint I hear from family members who are having difficulty getting along is, "We can't communicate with one another." The need for a child to be understood by his mother or father is probably one of the greatest emotional needs he has. At the same time, the satisfaction of the parent who feels understood by a child represents one of the greatest potential sources of adult happiness. Children want to be heard. Parents want children to understand.

One pleasure of my profession comes in seeing families mend previously broken ties. Those families that successfully go through the healing process always show an improvement in the way they talk and listen to one another. I remember one seven-year-old girl who had been the scourge of her home and school. After her parents made communication adjustments, she told me, "It feels good to talk and someone knows you're there."

A mistake we often make in assessing our communication with family members is to focus on the words that are exchanged. In fact, I sometimes ask a parent to say what they were thinking as their child talked. Often, the adult will admit, "I was thinking of what I was going to say once my child finished speaking."

Those parents who successfully communicate with their children do not always think of what they will say in response to the child's statement. Instead, they are thinking, *What is my child trying to tell me?*

In order to be effective in family relationships, it is important that parents pay heavy attention to all the messages being sent, both verbally and nonverbally, by the child. As we are able to set aside our own needs and focus on the needs of the child, we put ourselves in a better position to give the young person direction.

❖     ❖     ❖

Mrs. Pendleton could have reacted to Nelson's initial statement out of her own need rather than focusing on his need. When he came into the house and told of being "body slammed" by the bully next door, she could have become absorbed in any one of the following reactions:

- I'm not about to let any bully treat my son that way. Just let me get my hands on that kid!
- There's no telling what Nelson did to set himself up for a rough battle with that boy next door. You can't believe anything kids tell you.
- Oh, no! I hope Nelson's not hurt. Why do I allow him to play with those rough boys? Something like this is always happening.
- Why does Nelson have to bring all his problems to me? Can't he tell I have enough problems of my own?
- I'll just tell Nelson what to do. I've had plenty of experience dealing with similar situations. I can teach him a thing or two.
- I'll just ignore Nelson's whining, so he'll learn how to

take care of these things by himself. I don't want to get
involved.

Instead of reacting according to her own thoughts and emotions,
Mrs. Pendleton paid close attention to both the verbal and nonverbal
needs of her son. The note he left her later that evening was his way
of saying, "It sure feels good to be understood."

## UNDERSTANDING LEADS TO GOOD DECISION MAKING
Many parents have a tendency to step in too quickly with their own
solution to their child's problems. I believe one reason for this is that
most are not convinced that a child is fully capable of making wise
decisions without direct input from an adult. As we consider the most
important functions of parenthood, we can easily identify the need to
teach our children to use sound judgment. As we attempt to instill a
sense of reasoning in our children, we may be employing any of the
following tactics:

- Telling the child how he ought to handle a given situation.
  ("I would have given Luther a taste of his own medicine!")
- Taking the child's problem as our own and telling the child
  to watch as you fix things. ("Let's go outside right now.
  Where is Luther's mom? I want to talk to her.")
- Constantly reminding the child of what to do when he
  faces a difficult decision. ("Remember what I've told you to
  do when Luther treats you like that? Practice what we've
  talked about!")
- Encouraging the child to deny his feelings and simply
  act on his impulses. ("It's not going to do you any good to
  come crying to me. What are you going to do about your
  problem?")
- Becoming emotionally entangled in the feelings of the
  child. ("Oh, that's got to hurt. Come here and let Mom take
  care of you.")

These reactions (and others) send a message to the child: You
can't make independent decisions; you need to rely on me to make
decisions for you. While that may not be the parent's purpose, his

inability to step back and view matters as the child does can inhibit the child's growth in decision making.

Mrs. Pendleton responded to her son by showing that she saw the situation as he had. She said, "It hurts in a lot of different ways to be treated the way Luther treated you." That statement kept the words flowing from her son. After becoming convinced that his mother was on his side, Nelson sought comfort in the form of a hug. He later told her he appreciated her confidence in him with a loving note.

Nelson's behavior toward his mother was his way of stating, "Thanks for understanding me. That helps me make sense out of my problem. I can think more clearly when I know someone understands me."

## COMMUNICATION REQUIRES PERSONAL CONFIDENCE

As I talked with one mother about communicating with her children, she said, "I understand that I need to learn to listen to my children, but I'm afraid that if I don't throw in my thoughts, my kids will make poor choices." This mom and I talked of how she had become convinced that her children were not capable of making wise decisions. After she thought about it, she finally concluded, "I was never given the confidence of my parents to make independent choices. They always made most decisions for me. I guess I've learned to be the same way toward my own children."

Many of our communication skills are learned habits. An adult who had the childhood experience of constantly being told what to do or how to think may have difficulty making a shift to a communication style that calls for intense listening. Past experiences may have convinced us of any of the following beliefs:

- ◆ Children are not capable of making the right choice when given the opportunity to choose between right and wrong.
- ◆ A child is unaware of what his actual needs really are.
- ◆ Regardless of whether or not a child agrees with adults, he needs to appreciate what adults do for him.
- ◆ Children are self-centered and make choices based on their own needs, and don't weigh the needs of others.
- ◆ Children do not learn as much from the experiences of life as they do from the lessons taught by adults.

◆ A child is not in touch with his emotions. He does not really know how to express himself honestly.

Any of these adult beliefs can stand in the way of family communication. This failure to recognize the child's ability to make sense of his own thoughts and emotions is frequently a result of the adult's own past history of communication failure with adults. An adult's insistence on directing the communication with a child is often a reflection of the adult's lack of confidence in himself.

Mrs. Pendleton had the belief that her son could come to a stronger understanding of himself if he had a communication partner to help him wade through his thoughts and feelings. She knew that he might require guidelines as he made choices. But for him to learn to get along with others, he had to feel that the decisions he made were not forced on him, but were his own choice.

For example, after Nelson's mother asked him his plans, he could have said, "Luther needs to know how it feels to be 'body slammed.' I'm going back out there and show him what it's like."

Realizing that her son's action was based on a desire for revenge and not on common sense, Mrs. Pendleton could have said, "You're so mad at Luther, you want to hurt him. I think you should stay in the house for a few minutes before going back out." A disgruntled child would have pouted in the house, because his real desire was to punch out his neighbor. However, after his emotions had settled, his mother could have said, "You look a little calmer now, but I'll bet you're still mad about what Luther did to you."

A more subdued Nelson might then have said, "I am still mad at him. I'm not going back over there any more this week. I can't stand the way he acts so tough." His statement was evidence that he had accepted the limits his mother gave him and that he had made a better choice of how he would handle his problem. Avoiding the neighbor for a few days was a choice his mother could agree with. She knew the consequence of this decision would be more positive.

This mother had the confidence that her son could bring his emotions to a proper closing, but the early intensity of his feelings was a hint that the youngster needed boundaries around him. To have allowed the inexperienced child to act on his first angry impulse would certainly have meant further trouble. Once Nelson's anger was diminished, she trusted him to make a wiser choice, and he did.

### ❖ LISTENING UNLEASHES GROWTH ❖

King David had a close, intimate relationship with God. He wrote a moving acknowledgment of his heavenly Father's thorough knowledge of his thoughts and emotions:

> O LORD, you have searched me
> and you know me.
> You know when I sit and when I rise;
> you perceive my thoughts from afar.
> You discern my going out and my lying down;
> you are familiar with all my ways.
> Before a word is on my tongue
> you know it completely, O LORD.[1]

The closeness David felt to God was largely a result of God's ability to look deep within our souls and grasp the full meaning of the emotions and thoughts that cannot be adequately spoken. We all have inner sentiments that are not suitable for words. To know that we are so completely understood by God, who does not require words to know our feelings, can draw us closer to Him. As David felt near to his all-knowing heavenly Father, a child can have similar feelings about his insightful parent.

David concludes this prayer with the words, "Search me, O God, and know my heart; test me and know my anxious thoughts. See if there is any offensive way in me, and lead me in the way everlasting."[2] David's knowledge that he was wholly accepted caused him to want to be led by God into a fuller meaning of life.

As the parent shows the willingness to listen to all the child needs to express, the young person, like David, will want to be guided by his understanding parent. An accepted child who is asked, "How do you know your mother and father love you?" will invariably state, "Because they understand me." The parent's ability to step momentarily outside his own thoughts in order to experience those of his child draws the child closer to him.

As a parent learns to listen to his or her child, the child gains the following important messages:

- I trust you to learn to live cooperatively with others.
- Not only do I love what you do, I love who you are.
- I have no motives other than to do what is in your best interests.
- I believe that you can learn how to trust others the same way you have been shown trust.
- Despite our different positions in the family, you have equal importance and value to me.
- You can learn to make the choices that will serve you well into your adult years.

# ❖21❖

# *Examining*

❝**I** heard you use that phrase a few weeks ago, and it bothered me," Mrs. Hunter confessed.

"In what way did those words bother you?" I asked.

"I felt unsettled mostly because of what I might hear if I did what you suggested," was her answer.

The bothersome phrase I had used was *"Be bold enough to listen to yourself as you talk to your child."* The point being that if a parent listens to himself as the child would hear him, there are more than a few surprises in store for the parent. Often an adult is taken aback at the way a child interprets the words and gestures directed toward him.

I was interested in what experiences Mrs. Hunter had met as she tried my suggestion. As I asked her to elaborate, she could only laugh. "I almost hate to admit what I heard myself say to my son Justin that very day." She related a conversation that had taken place between herself and her fourteen-year-old son.

❖    ❖    ❖

Justin normally came home from school at about 4:15 each afternoon. It was his practice to ride home with an older boy who lived just a few houses down from the Hunter family. On this particular day, Justin was late arriving home. Mrs. Hunter had seen her neighbor's son drive by the house and knew that there must be some reason for her son's tardiness. She recalled thinking that Justin had better have a good excuse for being late, because she was worried about his well-being.

About thirty minutes after his normal arrival time, Justin sauntered into the house acting rather carefree about his tardiness. He had been dropped off by a young man Mrs. Hunter did not recognize. As soon as she saw her son, she demanded an explanation: "Young man, just where have you been? You're late! I've been worried sick about what might have happened to you. Don't you have any respect for me? Why didn't you call to let me know you'd be late? And who was that boy you rode home with? I don't know him."

Justin was floored by his mother's harsh tone of voice. Defending himself, he said, "Mom! I just stayed after school because Coach Ledford wanted me to look at some new equipment for pole vaulting. A salesman was there to show him what he had, and Coach wanted me to look at the poles before he ordered anything."

"Why didn't you call me to let me know where you were?" There was still a tone of anger in Mrs. Hunter's voice.

"I did call—twice! The phone was busy. I figured you wouldn't mind, so I stayed. I wasn't trying to do anything that would make you mad or anything like that!"

Mrs. Hunter was not through asking Justin questions. "Well, who was that boy you rode home with? You know I don't like you to ride with people I don't know."

"You've met him before. That was Mike Wilkins. He's the guy who won state last year in the pole vault. He told me he'd give me a ride home. I didn't think it would be such a big deal."

"Isn't he a senior? You know I don't like you riding in cars with boys three years older than you. Why do you do these things?"

By now Justin was tired of having to withstand his mother's scrutiny. "Mom, would you please leave me alone? Look, I'm sorry I didn't let you know where I'd be. I tried, but I couldn't get you, so I did what I thought you would tell me I could do. You sure know how to drive a guy crazy, you know it?"

## SELF-STUDY TEACHES VALUABLE LESSONS

After Mrs. Hunter related her dialogue to me, I asked her to evaluate what she had learned from her experience. She told me, "I felt bad that I had jumped down Justin's throat so quickly. I knew I had made him mad when I shouldn't have. I decided I would listen to myself the way Justin had heard me."

This mother showed the insight she had gained from this exercise as she listed for me the following messages she felt Justin had been given:

- I assume that you are guilty of some kind of wrongdoing since you did not come home at your normal time.
- I plan to make you feel guilty for causing me to feel upset for the last thirty minutes.
- Any explanation you offer for your action will be rejected. You can't give me a good enough reason for your actions.
- If I'm upset, I want you to be upset, too.
- It's not safe for you to tell me your side of the story because I have an answer for every argument you could make.
- The plain, simple truth isn't good enough. Maybe you would get a more understanding reaction from me if you "dress up" your story.
- I don't trust you to make independent decisions even if you feel they are appropriate.

When a parent must confront a child, it is typically the design of the parent to teach a useful lesson to the inexperienced young person. However, the words we choose and the expressions we display often betray our intended communication. In Mrs. Hunter's case, she intended to teach her son to take caution in the decisions he made. She wanted the teen to learn to exercise good judgment.

Let's change the scenario between Justin and his mother so that Justin can receive his mother's intended message without also being injured by her frustration. As Mrs. Hunter sees the neighbor's son drive by without Justin, her thought could be, *Justin's made a change in plans. I'm not really happy to have to wait to find out what he's doing, but I have no better alternative than to be patient.*

As Justin comes into the house, Mrs. Hunter says, "Hi, son.

You're home later than usual. I hope things have gone well this afternoon."

Sensing his mother's openness, Justin reacts, "Sorry I didn't let you know where I was. I tried to call you, but the line was busy. I figured you wouldn't mind if I stayed late at school. Coach Ledford wanted me to look at pole vaulting equipment a salesman was showing him before he bought anything."

Seeing that her son had not erred in his judgment, Mrs. Hunter decided to wait until later to talk to him about riding home with older boys. Rather than criticize him for the decision to stay after school, she states, "I guess you made what you thought was the right choice. Tell me about the poles the coach ordered. . . ."

By listening to herself as Justin would listen to her, Mrs. Hunter created a completely different climate than in the previous scenario. Gone were the communications of doubt, judgment, shame, and guilt. In their place were suggestions of faith, trust, confidence, and respect. Listening to herself as her son did placed Mrs. Hunter in a position later to have a conversation with him about the concerns she had about choices he had made.

## SELF-EXAMINATION CREATES REALNESS

A statement a frustrated parent might make is, *My child does not appreciate all that I do for him.* I have come to believe that one major reason for a child's misunderstanding of his parent is the lack of harmony between what we adults actually say and what we intend to say. A rule of thumb in communication states that our nonverbal exchanges take priority over—that is, they are received more clearly than—the words we say.

This rule tells us that when we want to convey a certain message to a child, it is of utmost importance that we be aware of what we are also saying through our behavior, tone of voice, and posture. The messages we send in these ways may take away from the importance of our words. We must make sure that our words, actions, and emotions are in line with one another.

As Mrs. Hunter and I talked of this communication guideline, she voiced her frustration: "That's an uphill battle for me. I have a hard time keeping my emotions out of the way when I want to tell Justin something I feel is important." I agreed that it is a battle for virtually all of us to meet this guideline.

One reason for this struggle is that few of us are taught during our early years that it is safe to say exactly what we think or feel. Parents typically teach children at a very early age to disguise their deepest feelings. Many adults do not recall receiving the kind of consistent patient parental reaction that encourages honest communication. Their past was frequently marked by the kind of give and take that pushed open communication underground. Unable to fully express what they felt in childhood, they become parents without having properly developed a valuable communication tool. It is difficult, then, for those parents to know how to match their verbal messages to what may be communicated nonverbally. This limits their ability to draw open communication from their own children.

A task of adulthood, then, is to become aware of the ways our nonverbal communication exercises veto power over the words we say. Ways we may erase the intent of our words through our nonverbal actions include:

- ◆ Failing to back up words with action. *Nonverbal message:* I'm betting that you will not recognize my inconsistencies.

- ◆ Masking our true thoughts under a thin veil of spoken sarcasm. *Nonverbal message:* I don't appreciate your need to be treated with respect.

- ◆ Adding extra emotion to the tone of voice. *Nonverbal message:* If I don't emphasize my words, you're likely to miss their value. *Or,* I want you to think this is more important to me than it really is.

- ◆ Displaying an emotionally cold or aloof attitude to try to elicit respect. *Nonverbal message:* I don't value you enough to become personally involved.

- ◆ Repeating a thought over and over to emphasize its importance. *Nonverbal message:* I think you're not smart enough to figure out something the first time.

♦ Dressing up a message with "colorful" adjectives. *Nonverbal message:* Unless I do more than is necessary, you won't catch the meaning.

When our verbal and nonverbal communication send identical messages, children learn to trust what we say to them. They come to see that we are genuine in our feelings for them. I enjoy hearing young people say, "I know I can count on my mom and dad to be up front with me. When they tell me something, I know it's the real thing."

Being genuine with our children involves three things: (1) saying what we mean, (2) meaning what we say, and (3) saying it in a way that preserves the child's feeling of worth. A parent cannot act genuine, for the child will recognize it as just that—an act. The parent must *be* genuine.

### ❖ EXAMINING OURSELVES IMPROVES RELATIONSHIPS ❖

Jesus used some of His harshest words to reprimand those who sought to change others, but failed to look within at their own need for improvement. He stated, "Why do you look at the speck of sawdust in your brother's eye and pay no attention to the plank in your own eye? How can you say to your brother, 'Let me take the speck out of your eye,' when all the time there is a plank in your own eye? You hypocrite, first take the plank out of your own eye, and then you will see clearly to remove the speck from your brother's eye."[1]

Jesus addressed a problem that applies to all relationships—the need to be genuine. Of course, in His language Christ is making an overstatement. I would think that as He spoke these words, those who heard Him poked each other and laughed at the ridiculous thought of a person with a huge log in his eye trying to find a tiny speck in another's eye. They got the message, though: *Before we attempt to make changes in others, we should first make certain that we are working to correct our own faults.*

In my own pilgrimage through life, I attempt to make a daily inventory of the progress I am making in my personal growth. I have learned that on the day I decide I have learned it all, I will have lost all possibility of being a healthy influence on my family members and others I love. A true mark of love toward our children states, *I love you enough to always look for ways I can grow to be a better person.*

After several weeks of concerted effort to be a genuine person, Mrs. Hunter told me, "You know, Lee, I have experienced more satisfaction over the last few weeks than I've felt in a long time." When I asked her to elaborate on that thought she added, "I know that I'm being totally honest with my family. I don't have the frustration I used to feel when I tried too hard to force my feelings on Justin and others. Because I'm listening to myself better, other people are hearing what I have to say."

This parent had caught the meaning of Jesus' words to first take the log out of her own eye before looking for specks in the eyes of others. She focused on self-growth and found the pleasant reaction of others to be a byproduct of her effort. I am convinced that when we change our words from "I'm saying this for your own good" to "I'm listening to myself for your good" our relationships with others become more satisfying.

CHAPTER

## ❖22❖

# *Influencing*

For the third time in just a few days, Heather had forgotten to put her dirty clothes in the clothes hamper. Her mother was tired of constantly reminding her to take care of this simple duty. One more time she jogged the forgetful child's memory: "Heather, how many times have I told you to put your dirty clothes in the hamper? I can't tell which clothes to wash unless you cooperate with me. Can't you do this one simple thing for me?"

An unconcerned response returned from Heather: "Oh, yeah, I forgot. I'll get them in just a second."

"Now, Heather!"

Heather made her way back to her bedroom where dirty clothes were strewn around the room. She started to complete her chore and gathered a few items in her arms, but quickly became interested in something else and dropped the pile, leaving her duty undone—again!

Assuming that her daughter had done as she had been told, Mother was dumbfounded when she entered Heather's room later only to find it in pretty much the same condition as it had been. Mom's initial desire was to find Heather and strangle her, or at

179

least give her a second scolding. Instead, she said to herself, "I'm not going to let that girl get the best of me. If she refuses to put her clothes in the hamper, then I'll refuse to wash them. She'll just have to wear dirty clothes." Satisfied that she was not going to lose this battle, Mom walked out of her daughter's room, resisting the urge to argue with her child.

Two days later Mom still held firm to her promise to herself to stay out of arguments with Heather over her dirty clothes. She smiled to herself when she noticed Heather was wearing a pair of dirty jeans to school. Internally she mused, "I'll bet her friends at school will say something about her dirty jeans. Maybe that will encourage her to put her clothes in the hamper so they can be washed." To Mom's dismay, Heather seemed unfazed at having to wear dirty jeans.

Two days later Heather asked her mother, "Mom, do you know if I have any clean underwear? I'm out."

Mom thought this would be the day Heather gave in and fulfilled her duty of picking up her dirty clothes. "Honey, I always put your clean underwear in your top drawer. If there aren't any in there, I guess they're all dirty." She waited for Heather's reaction.

As Heather appeared for breakfast a few minutes later, Mom asked curiously, "So what did you do about finding clean underwear?" She hoped the child would beg her to wash some clothes for her.

"I had to wear what I had on yesterday."

"You what?! Heather, you can't wear dirty underwear! That's downright disgusting!"

"But Mom," insisted the contented child, "that's all I have. You didn't wash any for me."

"I'll tell you why I didn't wash any underwear for you. You refuse to clean up your room. That's why! You have left dirty clothes on your floor for days now, and I refuse to clean up that pigsty you call a bedroom. If you want to wear clean underwear, you get into your room and pick up those dirty clothes! Now!"

"But Mom. . . ."

"Now!"

## BEING IN CHARGE ISN'T EASY

It is common for parents to feel totally exasperated at their inability to exercise control over their child's behavior. If children were left to their own choices, their tendency would be to make the kind of poor decisions that would result in one disaster after another. Someone needs to be in charge of the family. Of course, that person is the parent.

*Control* is a concept most of us have difficulty with when it comes to relationships. When we try to control the behavior of a child, a common result of our effort is to feel out of control. The harder we try to exert control over a child, the worse his or her behavior often seems to become. Consider the following family situations:

◆ Even though he is an intelligent child, Franklin makes an "F" for his midterm grade in English. To encourage him to study harder during the next few weeks of school, his parents ground him until he brings home a passing English grade on the next report card.

◆ Amy has gotten into a bad habit of talking ugly toward her mother. Tired of her daughter's disrespectful behavior, Mother tells Amy she may not watch a TV show she had been looking forward to seeing.

◆ Two brothers, Luke and Larry, have been at each other's throats all day long. Hoping to teach the boys a lesson in cooperation, their dad says they must spend an entire afternoon working together on a joint project. He assures them that any arguing will result in further "joint punishment."

◆ Knowing that Dee Ann has snuck out of the house recently, her parents decide to catch her in the act of misconduct. On a night they suspect that she plans to sneak out, the adults lay awake in their bedroom waiting to catch their unsuspecting daughter. After catching her red-handed, they issue a stiff punishment.

In each of these scenarios, the aim of the parents is to control a child who has shown poor judgment in decision making. The adults hope that by exercising control the child will recognize his error and change directions. No one can fault the intent of parents who look for ways to safeguard those things that are in a child's best interest.

But, in almost any family, children respond to controlling adults with a certain amount of skepticism. Unsure that their parents are fully aware of their needs, children will often strike back. For example:

- Upon learning that he has been grounded for making a poor grade in his English class, Franklin puts forth enough effort to pass that class. However, at the same time, he deliberately fails his math class. When his parents ground him for that low grade, Franklin accuses them of being unfair: "You said I wouldn't be grounded if I brought my English grade up, and I did. It's not fair!"

- Angry at her mom for not allowing her to watch her pre- ferred TV show, Amy refuses to talk to her mom at all. She says to herself, "If Mom is mad because she doesn't like the way I talk to her, then I just won't say anything. Let's see how she likes that!"

- While being forced to work cooperatively with one another by their father, Luke and Larry hardly look at one another as they complete their task. Each puts forth a minimal effort in finishing their chore. The next day while their dad is away from home, the two boys have another big fight.

- Caught by her parents as she slips out of the house late at night, Dee Ann heatedly accuses them of being "unfair." As her parents try to use logic in defending their desire to keep her from harm, she insists on pointing out their underhanded ways of trying to catch her.

CHILDREN KNOW HOW TO CONTROL

Children and teenagers like to feel that they are in control of their own lives. They enjoy knowing that they have a voice in the outcome of their own decisions. When a young person feels too much pressure from his parents to control his life, he fights back in an effort to regain some semblance of control over himself.

The tactics a child uses to control the family are different from the tactics used by adults. A child cannot tell his parents, "You're grounded!" He cannot take his mother's car keys and keep her from driving. A young person cannot say to her father, "I will not allow you to play golf with your friends this afternoon." Children have a different method of controlling adults, and I have to add, it is effective. Children learn at a very early age that by manipulating the emotions of a parent, they have effectively taken charge of that adult.

❖     ❖     ❖

Looking back at our illustration of Heather and her unclean room, we can see her control tactics in action. Heather recognized all the signs indicating her mother was trying to place controls around her. Her mother's reminders, threats, and pleas were reactions Heather had learned how to dispel. She responded to her mom by acting indifferent to her words. Her hope was that by ignoring her mother's guidelines one of several things would happen:

- Mom might give up on Heather and clean her room for her.
- Mom might relax her standards and compromise with Heather.
- If Mom insisted on having things her way, she would become exasperated at Heather's procrastination and be more upset than Heather.

In any event, Heather would know that she was in control of the home. She received confirmation of her position of power when her mom exploded at the thought of Heather wearing dirty underwear. At that point, Heather knew that nothing Mom did could take away the control the girl had successfully seized. She was in charge of her mother's emotions. Regardless of what happened next, Heather was certain that the real power of the home had been laid right in her lap!

### ❖ WINNING COOPERATION THROUGH INFLUENCE ❖

I have talked with many frustrated parents who have come to the dismal conclusion that their child is not fully under their control. The knee-jerk reaction of adults is to reach back for all the strength that can be mustered to force a sense of control over a family in a spiraling pattern. Quickly noticing he has the adults on the run, a young person will fend off all attempts to dethrone him—even if his "success" means the loss of valuable family relationships.

Most adults tell me that when they are under the fire of a child who will not give in to their leadership, they resort to the same methods that were shown to them when they were children. A common thought is, *I didn't act the way my child did because my parents wouldn't have put up with it. I would have been quickly put in my place.*

Most parents are convinced that the children of today do not respect adults in quite the same way that was true even one generation ago. Our world constantly encourages children to put themselves first, even at the expense of valued relationships. They are told that it is all right to express their emotions in an uninhibited style. Individual rights are often pushed in front of the good of others, including the family.

In addition to the mood of the times, I find that adults tend to forget the distasteful aftereffect of being harshly controlled by their own parents. One man told me bluntly, "I recall being backhanded by my dad whenever I did something he didn't like. I was pretty quick to mind him, not because I respected his way of disciplining me, but because I was afraid of him. Now that I'm a parent, I get frustrated when my child won't obey me. I find myself using the same kind of force. I don't know why, but I hope that maybe it will strike respect for me into my child."

One reality of human relationships is that we cannot force control over another person—not even a child. We can only influence a child to cooperate. The Bible gives this instruction to fathers, "Do not exasperate your children; instead, bring them up in the training and instruction of the Lord."[1] The wisdom of these words is that when we as parents instruct our children with the love and patience that characterizes Christ, we have a great influence over the young person.

I believe the relationship of a parent and child mirrors the relationship between God and humankind. There is nothing a child of God can do to separate himself from the love of God.[2] Yet, each person has the choice of living in that love or rejecting it. Similarly, parents' love for a child is enduring. The child, though, must decide whether to live within the love shown by his parents or seek affirmation elsewhere.

Biblical guidelines teach us that, while we cannot force control on a child, parental leadership can encourage the child to want to follow. The parent who attempts to influence rather than control the young person has many of these qualities:

- Spends time regularly in activities that are of interest to the child.
- Listens to the feelings of the child and withholds opinions when it is evident the child is not open to advice.
- Displays affection by frequently touching the child in ways that say, "I love you."
- Allows the child to disagree with decisions that have been made, but holds firm to what is right for the child.
- Avoids using emotions such as anger, guilt, shame, or fear as ways of forcing a child's behavior.
- Seeks the child's opinion on matters that affect the family.
- Frequently recognizes the good things the child does, even if those victories are small.
- Looks on the bright side of situations with the belief that good can come from any circumstance.
- Openly accepts criticism from others in an effort to become all God intended.
- Refuses to feel personally offended by the child's mistakes since they are a part of the growing process.

The one thing a parent does have control over is his own effort to place a priority on the behavior he displays toward his child. When the apostle Paul speaks of a parent "training" the child, it is with the understanding that training involves not only discipline but also positive teaching and acting as a strong role model.

Unfortunately, children may force parents to be more authoritarian than they would wish to be. A child who refuses to pick up dirty clothes, or shows disrespect, or blatantly violates curfew seems to push the parent out of a role of positive influence into a role of authority. However, it is not necessary to slip away from the guidelines we have discussed even when the child is especially difficult.

The parent may be required to act more quickly, be more decisive, and be less flexible than with a child who more readily complies with parents' requests. Yet, the urge to *force* change in the child must be resisted.

When the parent's focus is on those things under his power—words spoken to the child, time spent with the child, affirmation offered, and emotional restraint displayed—he finds that he can influence the child toward positive behaviors. Feeling no struggle to wrestle control from his parents, the child finds himself wanting to cooperate rather than compete with his parents.

CHAPTER

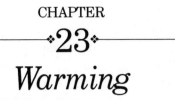

# Warming

Wendel was tired after a hard day at work—yet another in a long line of busy days. He had been put in charge of a demanding project that required all the energy he could muster. As Wendel and a coworker left the building at the end of the day, his companion joked, "I'm glad today's behind us. Now, if only I didn't have to go home to face my wife and those wild kids of mine, the evening would be perfect." Wendel smiled with his friend, but knew there was sincerity in the complaint.

When Wendel turned into his driveway, he was met by his son, Wayne, who was carrying two baseball gloves and a ball. "Hey, Dad. Wanna play catch with me?"

Dad was tired, but Wayne's enthusiasm gave him a lift. Wendel put his arm around his son and squeezed tightly. "Hey, big fella. So, you want to play a little baseball before we eat? How about coming into the house with me first? Give me just ten minutes to say hi to Mom and Wendy, and then we can spend a few minutes playing before supper."

Finding it easier now to put his thoughts of work behind him, Wendel went into the house. He sought out Wendy, who was busy playing the piano, and kissed her on the cheek as she continued to play. "Hi, Dad," she smiled, while not missing a note. He then found his wife and gave her a friendly greeting as he readied himself to play catch with Wayne.

Wayne was anxiously waiting for his father and boasted that his fastball was getting nearly as good as Nolan Ryan's. "We'll see about that," said Wendel as the two made their way outside. After they had been outside just a few minutes, Wendy appeared with her baseball glove. She wanted to be in on the fun. Wayne protested, but Wendel intervened and included his daughter in their activity.

"I'll be the catcher and each of you can take turns pitching to me," Dad suggested. Wayne and Wendy enjoyed a couple "innings" of baseball with their father before all were called in by Mom.

That evening, after Wendel had taken care of some personal business, he supervised as the children completed their home-work assignments. Later, he made sure the kids bathed themselves properly and helped them get ready for bed. He and Mom both spent a few minutes talking individually with Wayne and Wendy before the children went to sleep for the night.

In the course of only a couple hours, Wendel had said a lot to his children about their immense value to him. His communication with his family could only be described as "warm"—the way he touched his children, his tone of voice, the attention he offered, and his involve-ment in even the most mundane tasks spoke volumes of his commit-ment to his kids.

## WARMTH IS A COMMUNICATION DEVICE

I have known people who can accurately state, "I know and under-stand everything my child experiences. I know my child inside and out." Yet despite this understanding, some parents do not have good communication with their children. For family relationships to be complete, the understanding a parent has of a child must be com-municated. As we have seen, verbal communication is only one small part of the way we interact with others.

An important ingredient in the kind of self-growth that results in satisfying relationships with our children is an awareness of the nonverbal ways we communicate. A child can quickly determine if he is in the presence of someone who has genuine feelings of affection for him. Likewise, a young person is fast to note those signs of insincerity that tell of an adult's lack of authentic concern.

Note the following ways in which an adult can act in a way that satisfies a need of the child, but fails to communicate a warm feeling for the child:

- Just a toddler, Jerrod asks his father to help him put on his shoes. Perturbed at the intrusion, Dad takes Jerrod's shoes and mumbles, "Stick your foot up here, and let's get these things on." As he completes this job, he does not talk to Jerrod and only faintly hides his chagrin.

- When Mother finds out that her child, Dorothy, has homework to do, she reminds her daughter repeatedly to complete her assignments. Dorothy complains, "Mom, you don't have to talk to me that way. I'm going to get my homework done." Her mother snaps back, "You'd better. You can be sure that you'll be punished if you leave this house tomorrow without your homework completed."

- Troy and Jon are busy decorating the family room to surprise their mother on her birthday. They want their dad to share in their enthusiasm. He's reading a magazine in another room. After several requests for help, he makes a lackadaisical effort to assist the boys.

- Mom has a strict rule that food is not allowed outside of the kitchen. Her daughter has a friend over and takes apple slices into the living room to share with her companion. Wanting her daughter to respect the rules, Mom yells, "Tricia, you two get that food out of the living room. You know I don't want a mess on the furniture!"

Each of these parents would agree that he or she desires to teach responsible behavior to the child. Each adult can accurately make the statement, "I was doing what it takes to fulfill my obligations to my child." It is true, these adults did fulfill the letter of the law stating that when children need help, direction, or supervision, the parent should provide leadership.

Children do not pay close attention to the fact that their father or mother has fulfilled their parental obligations, though. They keenly focus on the spirit with which the parent acts. The parent's unspoken communication gives the young person an indication of how important he is as a member of his family.

## WHAT'S YOUR NONVERBAL COMMUNICATION STYLE?

A father once told me, "I know I'm rough on my kids. My mother and father were both hard on me, but I turned out all right—I guess."

This man's son was present when his father made this statement. The look of disbelief on the boy's face spoke a thousand words. I later asked this young man to explain his facial expression. He said, "If my dad thinks he learned the right way to handle kids because of the way my grandparents treated him, he needs to think again. I behave, all right, but it's not because I want to. I'm afraid of what he would do to me if I misbehaved."

This father had made the assumption that because his son showed good manners in public, it was only logical that his way of parenting must be right. As people often do, he had overlooked the nonverbal signals he sent to his son. At the same time, he missed the silent message of despair his son sent to him.

I often tell parents to take an inventory of the way they and their children send unspoken messages to one another. A helpful set of exercises parents can regularly follow is outlined here:

- Take advantage of opportunities to observe your child as he communicates with others. How well does your child attend to what others say to him? How forcefully does he make statements through his behavior?

- Note the way your child makes statements simply through her posture. A slouched posture may suggest a lack of interest. A rigid pose may indicate stubbornness. An eager position may show enthusiasm.

- Pay attention to whether your child's words and tone of voice match up. A child may verbally say, "Okay, I'm ready to help." Her nonverbal message, however, may be, "I'm going to help, but I refuse to do my best."

- ◆ Observe what your child says about himself in the way he dresses and grooms himself. Too much attention to outward appearance may say, "I need to stand out and receive recognition from others." Too little attention to these details may suggest, "It doesn't matter what people think of me. I'm at the bottom of the heap anyway."

- ◆ Now take the opportunity to observe yourself in the same ways you are learning to view your child. What do you say to others through your listening habits, tone of voice, emotional expressions, and outward appearance?

- ◆ When the opportunity is available, ask your child about his interpretation of your nonverbal style of relating to him. Refrain from the urge to defend yourself from any criticism you hear. Use the information to build on the strengths you are already developing.

Although communication is the most important aid to relationships we have, communication skills are often undeveloped. As we grow up, we do not always get a lot of feedback from others about the nonverbal messages we send. Since we cannot observe ourselves as we interact with others, we must seek information from others about how we affect them by the way we express our thoughts and feelings. Those who have grown up in a home where little emphasis was given to the unspoken communication of the family may be unaware of how they are perceived by those with whom they talk.

The signs of warmth sent between family members vary greatly from one family to another. A friendly verbal jab in one family may be considered a putdown in another family. Different words and gestures have varied meanings to individuals. Even within the same family, members may interpret words and signals from one another in different ways depending upon their temperament style or unique experiences. The parent is in the position to direct the flow of positive communication throughout the home. This leadership task begins with a working knowledge of how our communication efforts are accepted by others.

## ❖ WARM THEM WITH YOUR LOVE ❖

I enjoy studying the character makeup of Jesus. As I read scriptural accounts of Jesus' words and actions, I find myself trying to visualize the depicted situation as it must have been when it actually occurred. We do not have many recorded accounts of Jesus' interaction with children. However, Matthew told in his gospel of a time when Christ's disciples attempted to push away a group of children. Mothers had brought the children to be blessed by Jesus. Jesus noticed the commotion caused by this apparent confrontation. In words that have become well-known, Jesus softly said, "Let the little children come to me, and do not hinder them, for the kingdom of heaven belongs to such as these."[1]

We can only imagine the nonverbal signs of warmth shown by Christ to these young people. Certainly, as He held these children, the message in His touch said, "I accept you just the way you are." His facial expressions as the children talked to Him and asked questions said, "I am interested in all you have to say. Even the smallest detail is significant to Me." His gestures and posture must have said, "You can trust Me when I tell you what I think of you."

One lesson that all parents learn is that children are young and impressionable for only a short period of time. At a magic point in time each child makes a conscious decision to accept or reject the influence his parents wish to exercise over him. The interest Jesus had in the children brought to Him and His communication with them parallels the magnitude of the relationship a parent has to his or her children.

A wise parent chooses to extend his influence over his child by sending messages of warmth to the child, which like a magnet draw the child to the side of the adult. If the parent is to have the opportunity to guide his child to experience the kind of lifestyle that will bring happiness, he must use the kind of communication that states a commitment to family relationships.

❖        ❖        ❖

I was with Wendel, who was introduced at the outset of this chapter, when he was given a compliment about his children by another parent. In the style that characterized Wendel, he graciously accepted his friend's words of praise. After Wendel left our presence, this person thought aloud, "I wonder what his secret is that makes his children seem so close to him?" There was really no secret to Wendel's relationship with his children. He was a warm person whose communication with them made it clear how he felt about them.

# ❖24❖

# *Separating*

**"I**'ll do whatever you tell me to do," said Mrs. Preston. "Just give me your best advise, and I'll follow it." This mom spoke anxiously to me about her daughter, Tina. She was very concerned. Seven-year-old Tina had been to see a number of doctors because of constant complaints of physical discomfort. None of the doctors could identify a physical cause for her stomachaches, headaches, low-grade fever, and other assorted ailments. All had told Mrs. Preston that perhaps her daughter could not handle stress well. Mrs. Preston came to me as a last resort, thinking that maybe emotional problems were at the root of Tina's physical discomfort.

I was aware that this concerned mom wanted only what was best for her daughter and was looking for the right response that would "cure" her daughter of her ills. Wanting to keep the responsibility for change with Mrs. Preston, I had this reaction to her plea: "Let's look at what has already been done to help Tina and add to it."

Taking a quick mental inventory of her past efforts with her daughter, Mrs. Preston thought aloud: "Well, I've tried ignoring Tina when she complains of feeling sick. Her complaints seem so real, though, that I can't overlook them, so I end up giving her medicine or taking her to the doctor. I went through a stage when I scolded her for complaining so much, but I felt so guilty, I'd apologize and give her what she wanted. I tried putting her on a strict diet, thinking that maybe if she ate healthy foods she wouldn't get sick so often." Shrugging her shoulders, she sighed, "I don't know. I've tried just about everything, but she always seems to convince me that I need to help her."

I reacted to Mrs. Preston by saying, "Tina just won't let you have a life to yourself, will she?"

No sooner had the words come out of my mouth, when Mrs. Preston remarked, "You know, Lee, that's probably most of my problem. Do you think she uses her illnesses to manipulate me?"

"It does seem that your life and her life are wrapped pretty tightly together." I wanted this mom to continue with her thoughts.

Mrs. Preston stared blankly ahead for a moment. The look on her face suggested that she had known for quite some time that a greater distance would have to develop between them before Tina could overcome her frequent illnesses. Collecting her thoughts, she concluded, "That's probably where we need to start. I need to learn to live my life apart from Tina. I've just gotten too close to her."

"You know, Penny, it seems odd to think that a mother and daughter could be too close to one another, but there are times when two lives run together into one."

"And then you have a tangled mess," Mrs. Preston added.

## IT TAKES STRENGTH TO BE SEPARATE
In just a few moments, Mrs. Preston reached a conclusion that she had actively resisted for several years. She concluded that the missing element in helping her daughter overcome a problem was one of maintaining a separate life from her daughter.

When Tina was a baby, Mr. and Mrs. Preston had pinned all their hopes for happiness on their only child. Their marriage was not a happy one, but both hoped in vain that a child would bring meaning to their marriage. Not only did the child's presence fail to solidify the failing marriage, Tina's chronic demands made the split wider between the couple. Mrs. Preston found herself living through the life of her child to avoid the painful realities of her unhappy marriage.

This young mother explained the reason for her tight emotional hold on Tina: "When I was young, my parents had an awful relationship and hung on to their marriage just for the sake of me and my brother. When I was twelve years old, they finally split. My mother was so confused, she had practically no time to spend with me or my brother. She went through two more marriages before I left home at age eighteen. I have been determined not to let my problems come between me and my child. I guess I went to the opposite extreme by holding on too tightly to Tina."

A parent can pin all her hopes on the life of a young child. While the child may appear to benefit from a lot of positive attention, too much attention can create an entanglement that becomes hard to separate. Here are a few examples of parents and children who fail to live separate lifestyles:

- At the age of six, a child enters school for the first time. His mother knew it would be difficult to see her last son leave her total care. She experienced emptiness for months beyond his entry into school. This went far beyond the separation pains a normal parent would feel. She literally felt as though she had lost a part of her own life because another adult was supervising her son most of the day.

- A father never missed any of his daughter's soccer games. In fact, his interest in her games was so keen that he could not bear to miss one. He became enthusiastically involved to the point that he often was lost in his own emotions. His excessive investment in his daughter's athletics became a source of embarrassment to the whole family.

- Whenever Jack made less than a high grade on a test in school, his parents became very upset with him. They knew he was an intelligent teenager and hoped he would live up to his potential so he could attend a good college. Jack reached the point where he hated school so much

that his grades suffered. He even wished he could quit
school altogether.

◆ By the time Heidi was thirteen her mom wanted her to
have a boyfriend. Heidi, however, was not especially interested in boys. Whenever Mom brought up the subject,
Heidi quickly turned the conversation to another topic.
Chagrined at her child's apparent lack of interest, Mom
continually forced the girl to answer questions about why
she didn't enjoy talking to boys.

In many ways it is natural and normal for a parent to live
through the life of her child. As in virtually all matters involving
relationships, a healthy balance should be maintained between the
investment a parent makes in the child's life and the room the child
is allowed for autonomy. Mrs. Preston told me that she felt guilty if
she did not absorb herself in her child's activities. Yet, the net result
was that Tina failed to accept responsibility for her own life. The girl
remained dependent on her mother when her need was to learn to
get along in her own world.

ENTANGLEMENT CAN HAVE DIRE CONSEQUENCES
I believe that perhaps the single most difficult task of the parent is to
keep a proper emotional distance from a child. Too much distance can
cause the young person to feel unloved, while too much involvement
can create doubt in the developing mind. Parents will often ask how
much attention is just right. I point to several guidelines as a way of
making this decision:

◆ Step back and watch your child's behavior as objectively as
possible. If you wish, make written notes about your obser-
vations. Pay special attention to the emotions that seem to
drive your child. Look for the unspoken meaning in your
child's behavior.

◆ Ask those who are close to you for their honest assess-
ment of your relationship to your child. If it appears that
others are hedging in their response to you, be specific in

the questions you ask. Do not turn away any responses you may receive. Store this information in the back of your mind so you can later work to make sense of it all.

◆ Pay close attention to your child's requests of you. If he wants you to do too much for him, he may be expressing doubt in himself. If he wants you to stay away from him, he may be showing a need for better communication.

◆ Constantly update your expectations of your child to meet his developmental capabilities. As your child grows older, his need for your help will change. Make sure you change with your young person.

◆ Take an inventory of your activities and those of your child. Make sure you have your own set of activities that allow you to pursue things you enjoy. Likewise, be sure your child is developing his own interests. Leave plenty of room for joint activities you can do together.

One consequence I see in families in which the lives of parents and children become entangled grows out of the child's need for independence. As children get older, it is natural that they will want to assume greater responsibility for their own decisions. A child who is burdened by a parent who cannot let go of her emotional need to live through the child may rebel, even if rebellion is not a part of the young person's inborn nature.

A parent who has experienced rebellion at the hands of a previously obedient child may feel betrayed. A couple whose son turned from an easygoing and enjoyable child to a sassy and unappreciative young person expressed their hurt to me: "We feel stunned that our son could do and say the things to us that he has in the last few months. All his life we were sure he was the one in our family we could count on to remain close to us. Now we're beginning to feel as though he is the most distant from us."

Their son did not want to be rid of his relationship with his parents. He told me that he simply wanted his parents to make adjustments to his changing needs. He felt as though they could not recognize his need for increased independence. His rebellious behavior was a crude signal of his desire to negotiate an improved relationship.

### ❖ THE PLEASURE OF HEALTHY SEPARATION ❖

The more we study the word *control*, the more we understand the impact of this need in our lives. Too often, we parents show our love to our children by trying to control them. Our intention is to make sure that our children develop the qualities we are convinced will serve them well as adults. It takes a special kind of love to show a child that we simply appreciate who he is. This kind of love requires the belief that, with our guidance (not control), a child is capable of making reasonable decisions. These scenarios demonstrate this kind of parental love:

- ◆ As Roger comes into the house, he is wearing a frown that says something has gone wrong. He complains, "I don't think I'll ever be good enough to play basketball with Joey and Calvin. They're always hogging the ball and won't give me a chance to shoot."

    His mother believed that Roger could learn from this frustrating experience. She responded to him by saying, "Joey and Calvin don't give you the credit you feel you deserve when you play basketball together. It would be nice to get the chance to prove yourself."

- ◆ Belinda feels shamed by her boyfriend who has betrayed her by telling others information that she thought was safe with him. After expressing her irritation, her dad remarked, "It makes you wonder where to draw the line when you want to tell someone something you don't want everyone to know. It hurts to know that even your boyfriend may not understand your need to keep certain thoughts private."

- ◆ Two sisters have been engaged in an ongoing battle over which one was responsible for making a mess in their bedroom. They bring their argument to their mother, hoping that she will solve the dispute. Of course, each girl also hopes that Mom will side with her. Instead, Mom says, "That's something you can work out between yourselves. Just remember our rule that when you argue you lose the privilege of certain freedoms."

In each of these situations, a parent showed love for a child not by trying to control the thoughts and actions of the young person, but by appreciating his or her ability to come to appropriate conclusions about personal needs. When a child feels this kind of approval from his parent, he comes to see himself as capable. His personality blossoms to become all he is capable of being. He does not feel that he is simply an extension of his controlling parent, but feels that he is a unique individual.

I talked once with a man in his twenties who had become a father for the first time. He reflected on his own upbringing and the relationship he had with his parents: "When I was young, I sometimes felt frustrated with my parents because they kept telling me I could make decisions on my own. I really wanted them to make those decisions for me. Now, though, I'm glad they kept their distance in that way. I learned how to handle just about any problem that came along."

It is especially tempting to make decisions for young children because we fear that they will make poor choices if given the freedom to draw their own conclusions. Yet, by providing healthy boundaries and then allowing the child to make choices within those limits, the result will be a child who is capable of being independent and responsible.

❖     ❖     ❖

Throughout his New Testament letters, Paul wrote of the personal qualities of those who have a strong impact on the lives of others. Paul wrote to the people in Philippi about the power that comes from being at peace with yourself. He encouraged his readers to "let your gentleness be evident to all." He saw the value of an attitude of inner peace, thankfulness, and the building of a heart and mind that are patterned after the example of Christ Jesus.

He explained further, "Whatever is true, whatever is noble, whatever is right, whatever is pure, whatever is lovely, whatever

202 Qualities of the Maturing Parent

is admirable—if anything is excellent or praiseworthy—think about such things." He concluded with this, "Whatever you have learned or received or heard from me, or seen in me—put it into practice. And the God of peace will be with you."[1]

Paul was telling his readers, whom he considered as his children, "I have found that when I focus my thoughts on those things that draw me closer to the goal God has in mind for me, I have a peace about myself and my relationships with others." Paul's inner satisfaction contributed to making him probably the most influential teacher in all of Christian history. He was an effective leader, not because he tried to control others, but because he was an encourager and brought out the best in others.

A parent who has the strength to be separate from his child can experience the greatest source of parental satisfaction. The child who is loved and appreciated for his strengths—and is not controlled—can bloom into his own unique self. In turn, the parent is also enriched.

CHAPTER

## ❖25❖

# *Relating*

"**I** really resent my dad for the way he treats me now that I'm an adult," stated thirty-five-year-old Landon.

"How's that?" I asked.

"He treats me so nice, as if I'm his equal," came the reply. At first this response appeared to me to be a mistake. How could a grown man resent the fact that his father treats him as his equal? Yet as Landon talked further, I realized there was a reason for his feelings.

"You see, when I was young I sometimes wondered if my dad even knew I existed," explained Landon. "There were days when he would come into the house and he didn't seem to notice that I was there. He just ignored me. My dad wasn't mean to me or anything like that, he just didn't seem to need to have much of a relationship with me while I was growing up."

"But now it seems strange to you that he has a strong interest in everything you do."

"Exactly! I feel as if he's taking credit for whatever I've done that's positive. It's as if he says to himself, 'That's my boy. He's the person he is today because of the way I raised him.' That's just not true. If anything, I've gotten where I am today in spite of the lack of attention I got from my father. I believe if it had not been for my mother, I never would have learned to believe in myself."

"Would a part of you like to tell your dad exactly what you think?"

"Yeah, but that wouldn't do any good," said Landon, summarizing his own thoughts. "I really doubt that my father would be able to understand how bothered I am that he wants to spend time with me now, but that he had no interest in me when I was younger."

"People can be blind to the effects of their past behavior," I stated, letting this man know I understood his feelings.

"You know, Lee, at least my childhood experiences taught me one thing above all others: I need to make sure that I spend plenty of time with my kids. When they grow up, I want them to look back and say, 'Even though my dad made some mistakes, at least I know his relationship with me was important to him.'"

## THE PARENT-CHILD RELATIONSHIP IS INVALUABLE

Parents often ask me what discipline tool I find most effective in controlling (there's that word again) my own children. I explain that there is no single technique that works in teaching children to reach their inner potential. In fact, discipline is not the way at all to inspire a child to grow emotionally or spiritually. When I find myself having difficulty within my own family, I immediately do a self-study to determine the status of my relationship to each of my daughters. My wife, Julie, and I have learned that when we have demonstrated to our children their importance in our lives, they have a strong desire to want to please us and follow our leadership.

I believe that important changes in a child's behavior cannot be made outside of a relationship that offers the child encouragement and a reason to keep moving forward. As we look at the dynamics in the family and the role of the parent, we can identify several guidelines that lead to satisfying changes in the growing child:

- The parent must make a priority of the time spent with each family member. There is no substitute for quality time in building a bond between parent and child.
- The parent should assume the leadership role in the relationship with the child, keeping in mind that leadership

means offering guidance, but not control, to the child.
- The parent's love for his child parallels the kind of love God has for His children—no strings attached.
- The parent makes every effort to understand life from the child's point of view, whether or not the child's viewpoints seem reasonable.
- Communication with the child is given top priority so the child can see that the parent does, in fact, understand him.

Note that in this list of guidelines there is no mention of discipline. Sure, there will be times when it is necessary and advisable to discipline a child, but that should not be the main tool in shaping his character. The kind of thinking I am suggesting is often seen as radical because it differs so much from the way most of us were raised. In most homes, guidelines for raising a responsible child were built around the authority of the adult, not the relationship between the parent and child.

## IT'S OKAY TO BE REAL IN FRONT OF YOUR CHILD

Sometimes we feel it is important to keep up a certain image in front of our children. We may be afraid that "letting our hair down" only offers the children the opportunity to take advantage of our weaknesses. Perhaps the most important quality of a parent is to be 100 percent real in the home. A parent is real when:

- There are no "masks" worn in front of the children.
- Inner feelings and outward actions match.
- Feelings and attitudes are expressed constructively to the child.
- Needs for personal improvement are not ignored.

Being real in front of the child has a way of opening communication within the family. Landon related the desires he had for his family: "I want to be more of a role model to my children than I had in my father. That sounds good when I say it, but I know it puts pressure on me to watch myself constantly to make sure I'm always working to make things better in my own life."

Being real with a child may mean the parent will express frustration, disappointment, annoyance, or any of a number of other emotions. The parent should not simply let his emotions explode, though, since it is also important that self-disclosure be handled appropriately. The parent should avoid sending the child the suggestion that it is the young person's fault that the parent feels as he does. Such a statement suggests intolerance on the part of the parent. The point is that the parent should be responsible for his feelings and not allow them to block a healthy parent-child relationship.

Examples of both open and intolerant exchanges toward a child are as follows:

> SITUATION: A child has just shown her mother a school test paper with an "F" on it. The child has suggested that her grade would have been higher if only Mom had helped more as she studied for the test.
> OPEN RESPONSE: "I know you're bothered by your low grade and even feel it might be partly my fault. It bothers me that you may feel I'm not willing to help you."
> INTOLERANT RESPONSE: "Hey! Don't blame me. You made that 'F' on your own. I can't go to school for you, you know!"

> SITUATION: Kevin has been asked to mow the front yard for the last three days. The grass really needs to be mowed. The parent brings the subject up again.
> OPEN RESPONSE: "Kevin, I know you're having a hard time getting around to mowing the yard. I have to admit, I'm having a hard time being patient with you."
> INTOLERANT RESPONSE: "Kevin, you've tried my patience about as long as I can stand! Get out there right now and mow that grass. I can't stand a lazy kid!"

> SITUATION: Angela has her heart set on being asked to a party by a boy she admires. Her mother thinks there is not a chance that the boy will invite her to go with him.
> OPEN RESPONSE: "Angela, I know how much you want to go to

the party with Jay. I'd be less than honest, though, if I encouraged you to plan on going with him."

**INTOLERANT RESPONSE:** "Angela, get real! Jay's not about to ask you to go to that party with him. He already has a girlfriend. You'd better make other plans."

A parent who is real is willing to share his feelings and emotions honestly. The adult has a heartfelt need to be genuine as the child is given the kind of feedback he needs. To be real with a child does not mean using the kind of aggressive reactions that put the young person on the defensive. The child's needs are taken into account, because a genuine parent wants to express himself in a way that will keep the lines of communication open.

## LET YOUR LOVE HAVE NO EXCEPTIONS

Landon thought aloud with me about his father: "He's not a bad man, but often I felt I had to be a certain kind of person before he accepted me. He likes me now that I'm an adult because I don't get in his way or cause him to have to put out any extra effort."

Knowing Landon's meaning, I added, "But it wasn't always that way between you and your father."

"No. When I was a boy, I felt that I was more of a nuisance to him than anything else."

"What convinced you of your father's feelings when you were a boy?" I asked.

"It took practically nothing for him to snap at me and tell me to quit doing whatever I was doing. It seemed that if I was bothering my dad, my behavior must have been wrong. Another thing that let me know where I stood with him was that he hardly ever asked me to do anything with him. He assumed I was not interested in his world, and I became convinced he wasn't interested in mine."

Wanting to know what Landon had come to believe about his self-worth, I commented, "You know, a lot of children assume that if their own father is not interested in them, then they must not have a lot of worth. Do you remember thinking something like that?"

Landon hung his head as those words came out of my mouth. The thought I had suggested was certainly familiar to him. "I simply assumed that I was tainted or something. I remember thinking that all my friends got more attention from their dads than I did, so that must make them better than me. To this day, I still have this empty feeling when I am around men my age who talk about their good relationships with their dads. It makes me feel like half a person."

Landon's dad had given him the message, "I'll accept you when you are an adult and no longer a burden to me." Many other adults have been given the same message, with the only difference being the specific condition for acceptance.

Something tragic happens when a parent puts conditions on his love for a child. As a child meets the demands of his parent, he loses something from himself. In most cases, as was true with Landon, that lost "something" is a personal sense of worth. By having to change to become something an adult could value, the child loses sight of his own importance.

Personal development has many ironic twists. One of the oddest is that, as a child feels pressure to fit a certain set of demands, he loses his ability to become acceptable to himself. Many reasons can be identified that a parent would want to put conditions on a child. For example:

- A father demanded obedience from his children when they were in public because he wanted the reputation of being in control of his family.
- A mother expected her children to be complimentary of her when she did anything for them because she needed reassurance that she was useful to someone.
- A child was catered to by both her parents and was given virtually anything she wanted. Her parents' giving nature suggested too strong a need to be liked.

By expecting obedience, compliments, and gratitude from their children, each of these parents was placing unnecessary conditions on their relationship. True commitment to the parent-child bond states, "I will accept you as you are so you will learn to accept yourself." That kind of love opens the child to the lesson that he is free to move through life without fear of risking family relationships simply because of the mistakes he will certainly make.

## ❖ GROW WITH YOUR CHILD ❖

The psalms record many of David's prayers. In one he wrote, "Search me, O God, and know my heart. . . . See if there is any offensive way in me and lead me in the way everlasting."[1] I believe David's attitude in this prayer is the desire of each child. As David wanted to experience the warmth of his heavenly Father, who understands all things, a child wants the same response from his parent.

Virtually any adult can identify many of the needs of a child. We can all state with accuracy that a young person needs to be provided his physical needs, offered rewarding support, and given daily interaction. The aim of the parent's understanding, though, is to lead the child to a greater knowledge of himself as he moves toward growth and completion as a person.

A parent who grows with her child seeks to model the relationship God has with each of us. The parent tries to go beyond a simple recognition of the child's thoughts and emotions by sensing the young person's feelings as if they were her own, without becoming lost in those feelings. By moving in the world of the child, as God does with us, the parent can communicate accurately to the child. She can even know those emotions of which the child is only faintly aware.

Some parents only know about their child. They have failed to grasp a complete meaning of who that child really is. Understanding a child involves a personal identification with the young person. God personally identifies with each of us. Yet because He maintains His separateness from us, He can also lead us, as so poetically requested by David. A parent who can grasp the inner world of the child is in a like position to lead the young person to make constructive and fulfilling changes.

# *Epilogue*

Life does not take a break. A mother of three children who had been through a difficult time in her own youth told me, "I wish time would stand still for just a few moments so I could learn how to handle the future of my own family." That would be a wonderful luxury, but unfortunately, we have to learn all we can while time moves along.

Family life contains one small event after another. Some of those events turn into crises. It is from the crises in our lives that I believe we can grow the most. Sadly, it is also from the crises of life that we may simultaneously receive the greatest hurt.

It has been my hope and aim to teach you some lessons that can be gleaned from your own journey through life. Even if you have endured the most difficult family traumas, you have within you the ability to profit from your past history. You can take the events your life has given you, learn all you can about your responsibilities in the present, and move forward toward a bright future.

To successfully reach the goal of satisfaction in family relationships, the parent needs more than love for her children. Understanding the past and its affect on the present is needed. The ability
to take what the past has given and build on that foundation, no
matter how weak or strong, is needed. Skills for handling the communication and management demands of the family are necessary.
I hope you have met some of these needs through reading the pages
of this book.

Let me encourage you to talk openly with other family members
and friends about the things you are learning about yourself. Much
of the personal growth we experience comes through the daily interaction we have with others. You may wish to form a study group with
other parents as a way of promoting an environment for learning as
well as an opportunity for mutual support.

A study guide for this book is offered in the appendix. Additionally, Rapha's Church and Family Resources Division offers the
vehicle for involvement in a more formal study program directed at
personal and spiritual growth. *Rapha's Handbook for Group Leaders*
gives details for meeting needs in this way. Involvement in study
groups allows individuals to share common beliefs and values freely,
demonstrate acceptance of one another, and relate common experiences in a supportive manner.

As I have written this book, I have brought to life encounters
from my counseling practice in the hope that the learning experiences of others may strike a healing chord in you.

*Aim for perfection, listen to my appeal, be of one mind, live in
peace. And the God of love and peace will be with you.*[1]

# About Rapha

Rapha Resources' books, workbooks, videos, and audio cassettes provide practical, biblically sound information and encouragement for people who struggle with family of origin issues, low self-esteem, codependency, sexual abuse, depression, eating disorders, chemical dependency, marriage and family issues, inordinate fear, and bitterness. These materials are designed to be used by individuals as well as in support groups. Excellent group leader's guides and training materials are also available.

Call (800)460-HOPE or (800)460-4673 for a free catalog.

APPENDIX

# Study Guide

## ❖ SESSION ONE ❖

**READ:** Chapters 1 and 2.
**OBJECTIVE:** To build a beginning understanding of the effects the past has on present family relationships.

DISCUSSION QUESTIONS
1. In what ways has your past influenced the way you view yourself as a parent?
2. In what ways do you try to control your past, even though it is not possible to change it?
3. What messages do you communicate to your family members that suggest you may not be tolerant of their emotional needs? Did aspects of your communication style result from past experience?
4. In what ways do parents become trapped in a pattern of negative communication, focusing mostly on the bad things children say or do?
5. In what ways does a child learn about trust through his parents' communication with him?

ASSIGNMENTS
1. Make a conscious effort to note how often you compliment your children. Also notice how frequently you criticize or discipline them. Work at offering at least two to three times as many positive words as negative.

2. Make a list of the ways you've failed to forgive yourself because of past mistakes. Begin the road to self-acceptance by learning to accept yourself in spite of past history.

BIBLICAL REFERENCE: 1 Thessalonians 5:12-15
The apostle Paul identifies for us many of the characteristics of effective leaders. Because as parents we are in leadership positions in the family, it is important to cultivate these qualities. We are most effective in our efforts to guide our children when we have acquired leadership traits children can admire.

## ❖ SESSION TWO ❖

READ: Chapters 3 and 4.
OBJECTIVE: To examine the impact of early family experiences on the way parents communicate.

DISCUSSION QUESTIONS
1. How can a family be hurt by poor communication, even though that communication is not necessarily quarrelsome?
2. When communication skills are not taught, how does a child go about showing others how she feels?
3. Is it possible for a child (or even an adult) to completely hide from others the emotions that are within him? How do you attempt to hide your emotions?
4. In what ways does your own unmet need to feel understood by others influence the way you listen to your child? What impact does your communication style have on the young person?
5. How does the emotion of fear influence the way a child attends to the statements made to her by an adult?

ASSIGNMENTS
1. The next time you have a disagreement with your child, take time later to allow your child to voice personal feelings to you. Even if you think your child is completely wrong in his or her interpretation of a situation, work to understand the child's point of view. Keep your thoughts to yourself.

2. Take note of the power your words have on family relationships. Notice how a few misplaced statements can cause hurt feelings. Practice using well-timed statements as a powerful healing ointment.

**BIBLICAL REFERENCE:** 1 Corinthians 3:10-15
The Bible offers instruction about the way each of us builds a foundation that will become the base for all that we do or say. As parents we are in a prime position to help our children build a stable foundation of relationship skills that will serve them well throughout life.

## ❖ SESSION THREE ❖

**READ:** Chapters 5, 6, and 7.
**OBJECTIVE:** To understand how the past can create unneeded feelings of low self-worth in parents.

DISCUSSION QUESTIONS
1. How can the denial of life's difficult circumstances eventually surface in the behavior of a young person? Is denial always bad? When does it become a negative force?
2. What happens to feelings that go "underground"? Do all feelings eventually come to the surface?
3. In what ways are the lifestyles of denial of personal needs and overindulgence similar?
4. How do emotions get out of hand when a child does not learn to examine the needs of both self and others?
5. How does a weak childhood self-esteem create problems later in an adult's family life?

ASSIGNMENTS
1. Watch what you do or say when another person compliments you. Take note whether your tendency is to reject the compliment or expect more praise. What does this say about your self-esteem?
2. Learn to be constructive when you offer instructions to your child. If you offer praise, be specific in your comments. If you

must offer criticism, be kind and make your statement as quickly as possible.

**BIBLICAL REFERENCE:** Psalm 19:14
This beautiful verse tells us that both the private thoughts and public statements we make are to be pure. The motives of our outward behavior are driven by the thoughts that occupy our heart and mind. In a cyclical fashion, our thoughts influence the way we relate to our children, which in turn impacts the way our children perceive themselves.

## ❖ SESSION FOUR ❖

**READ:** Part 2 introduction, chapters 8 and 11.
**OBJECTIVE:** To become more aware of the way parents display behaviors that are defenses against the past.

## DISCUSSION QUESTIONS

1. What stress can you identify from your past that continues to be a problem for you? How does it show in the way you relate to family members?
2. What drives parents to try to reason with a child when she is in need of redirection? In what ways does the child recognize the parents' attempts to reason with her as a chance to manipulate the adults?
3. In what ways do parents tend to interpret a child's actions in light of their own past history?
4. How can a child defeat parents who try to overpower him by the use of force or emotional intimidation?

## ASSIGNMENTS

1. The next time you have an argument or disagreement with your child, take time to reflect on the words that you and your child exchanged. Think of the message you intended to send to your child. Then think of the way your child interpreted your verbal expressions. How closely do your child's thoughts match your intended communication?
2. The next time your child suggests you are being inflexible—

directly or indirectly—stop your conversation immediately. Ask your child to give you his or her alternative solution to the problem at hand. If it is even remotely feasible, accept it without further discussion. Watch the reaction your child gives you. Discuss the situation with him or her at a later time.

**BIBLICAL REFERENCE:** Matthew 22:15-40
This account of repeated confrontations between Christ and religious leaders offers a wonderful example of how Jesus kept His communication with others from deteriorating into arguments. He not only chose His words carefully, He also refrained from engaging in useless verbal banter with those who disagreed with Him. His example of restraint can be followed by all of us in our dealings with family members.

### ❖ SESSION FIVE ❖

**READ:** Chapters 9 and 12.
**OBJECTIVE:** To learn how emotions that go "underground" can resurface in the form of family disruption.

### DISCUSSION QUESTIONS
1. How do certain emotions get such a bad reputation? Is the reputation of these emotions justified?
2. How does a child show he is aware of the emotions of his parent? How accurate are children in correctly identifying the feelings of adults?
3. How can the past inappropriately teach adults to be closed to the emotions that they feel within?
4. Why do adults deny the reality of some of life's most difficult circumstances? Is there ever a time when denial is helpful? When does this defense cease to be useful?
5. Does forgiveness include the need to agree with the wrong one person has forced on another? What does forgiveness involve?

### ASSIGNMENTS
1. Ask someone who knows you well to help you identify ways you take responsibility for the mistakes of others. Use this exercise

to study how you rationalize the way you react to others.
2. Do something for yourself this week. Even if it means you have to tell someone no, make time to do something special. As you feel renewed, you will find more energy to give to others.

**BIBLICAL REFERENCE:** 1 Corinthians 15:3-11
Paul would have had every reason to make excuses to cover his sordid past, which was marked by one act of aggression after another. Instead of excusing his past or denying its reality, he did what we all should do—he learned from it. Paul used his understanding of himself to became a positive influence on many lives.

### ❖ SESSION SIX ❖

**READ:** Chapter 10.
**OBJECTIVE:** To learn how the sensitive emotions of parents can be either hidden or overworked.

## DISCUSSION QUESTIONS
1. How can the decisiveness of adults disguise their actual sensitivity to the feelings of others?
2. How difficult is it to know when to be decisive and when to hold off on a decision until it can be thought out more thoroughly? What circumstances can help you to know when to respond to your child's needs?
3. How does listening help to take away the sting of having to make an unpopular decision?
4. In what ways are passive people like their more aggressive counterpart?
5. How do children react to parents who are either too strict or too lenient? Are there similarities in the two parenting response styles?

## ASSIGNMENTS
1. As you read the newspaper this week, look for articles about people who have been too aggressive in their behavior. Note how their insensitivity to others created harm. Find similar articles about people who were found guilty of crimes that

resulted from being too passive. Even though these accounts are likely to be extreme examples of the misuse of emotions, we can learn by observing the actions of others.
  2. If you make a mistake this week that involves your child, take the chance to say "I'm sorry." Refrain from tacking on an excuse for your behavior. Let your child have a turn to react to you.

**BIBLICAL REFERENCE:** James 3:1-12
James identifies some of the difficulties all of us have in knowing how to make our communication more meaningful. He tells us that while no one is perfect, we can all strive to make the most of the words we use to influence our children.

### ❖ SESSION SEVEN ❖

**READ:** Part 3 introduction and chapters 13 and 16.
**OBJECTIVE:** To learn how hope must be balanced with an expectation of accountability for a relationship to succeed.

DISCUSSION QUESTIONS
  1. How can adults deceive themselves that things will get better when evidence suggests otherwise?
  2. How can one spouse become dependent on the other in ways that are not healthy?
  3. How is a child adversely affected by having a parent who constantly rescues others from trouble? What lessons about relationships is a child likely to learn when parents are not realistic in their expectations for the family?
  4. How do frustrated relationships and loneliness influence one another?

ASSIGNMENTS
  1. Make a list of several frequent problems in your home. Make an honest evaluation of how much at fault you are for the situations. If you are at fault, strive to make changes. If you are not at fault, keep out of patterns in which you blame yourself unnecessarily.
  2. Set aside one night this week for you and your children to

spend time playing your favorite board games. Emphasize having a good time being together, no matter who wins or loses.

BIBLICAL REFERENCE: 1 Corinthians 13:4-13
In this well-known passage, Paul describes what it means for one person to love another. As we get older, we realize that love is not just an emotion, but an action. After he names the qualities of someone who demonstrates genuine love, he tells us of the way we should continue to grow in our understanding of this important emotion.

### ❖ SESSION EIGHT ❖

READ: Chapter 14.
OBJECTIVE: To learn how the adjustments parents make to the past can be passed on to the child.

DISCUSSION QUESTIONS
1. How much impact do you feel parents have on the development of behavioral traits in a child? How much of a child's behavior is a result of an inborn personality?
2. When a child does not know how to express emotions, how does he go about communicating personal needs?
3. What methods can a child use to "punish" parents that adults cannot use? What evidence does the child have that his efforts have been effective?
4. Do you think there is a relationship between childhood rebellion and family affluence? How might the two be connected?
5. What may encourage a young person to look for happiness in the accumulation of things?

ASSIGNMENTS
1. Take time in the near future to plan an activity in which your family does something for someone else. Use this as a springboard for your family to routinely seek opportunities to be giving of your time to others.
2. Concentrate on making your child feel important because of the time you spend with him or her rather than because of the things you give.

**BIBLICAL REFERENCE:** Matthew 19:23-30

These two things are given a high position of importance in today's society: power and material wealth. When we recognize that we can overemphasize these qualities to a harmful degree, we are well on the way to understanding the value of lasting relationships.

## ❖ SESSION NINE ❖

**READ:** Chapters 15 and 17.

**OBJECTIVE:** To observe a child's accuracy in interpreting the behavior of the parents.

### DISCUSSION QUESTIONS

1. How does a child imitate the behavior of her parents? What factors make a child likely to model the actions of her parents?
2. In what ways can parents' frustration contribute to a child's difficulty coping with the normal stresses of life?
3. In what ways are frustration and depression related? How are these emotions seen in a child's behavior?
4. How can the reactions of parents, even though well-intended, create feelings of doubt in a child?
5. What factors can encourage parents to be overly protective of a child? What effect does this have on the young person?

### ASSIGNMENTS

1. The next time your child comes to you with a problem, take time to listen to him or her express personal concerns to you. Hold off on making an immediate suggestion of what can be done to solve the problem. Leave that responsibility to your child.
2. Give yourself at least three compliments per day for the next week. Don't worry if it appears that you are too proud of yourself, as that's not your intent. It is important that you always remember your positive qualities.

**BIBLICAL REFERENCE:** Matthew 6:25-34

In this portion of the Sermon on the Mount, Christ addresses the

problem of worry and anxiety. Family patterns that have become out
of balance often indicate that the adults are attempting to relieve
their anxiety through overcorrection. Christ's words teach us that
when we take care of our daily family needs we are more likely to be
free from the need to worry.

### ❖ SESSION TEN ❖

**READ:** Chapters 18 and 19.
**OBJECTIVE:** To understand how parents can influence a child by
showing emotional control.

## DISCUSSION QUESTIONS
1. How do adults typically try to maintain control of the family?
   What can a child do, even at a young age, to try to wrestle control away from the parents?
2. How can a child tell that he is gaining control of the family?
   What cues do parents give to let the child know he is succeed-
   ing in taking charge of the home?
3. How can a child who has been shown inappropriate love and
   freedom in her early years change from a compliant child to
   one who is demanding and self-centered?
4. What might parents do that could keep a child from learning
   through the experiences of life?
5. How does society encourage young people to be self-centered?
   What problems does this create for the family?

## ASSIGNMENTS
1. Hold a family council meeting one day this week. Have each
   person decide on a favor he or she can do for another family
   member. Use this activity as a springboard for a discussion
   of how the family functions best when each member looks for
   opportunities to help the others.
2. Offer your services to your child for one hour this week. Tell
   him or her that during that hour you will complete any reasonable chore that is assigned to you. Work hard during that hour.
   Concentrate on communicating to your child that you want to
   do the best job you possibly can.

**BIBLICAL REFERENCE:** Galatians 5:16-26
This passage contrasts the lifestyles of those who live according to the "flesh" and those who live according to the "spirit." The first list of characteristics centers around meeting selfish desires, while the second list is more relationship oriented. We gain greater satisfaction when we give of ourselves to others. We also see positive results when we use a positive relationship as a way of influencing others.

❖ **SESSION ELEVEN** ❖

**READ:** Part 4 introduction, chapters 20 and 21.
**OBJECTIVE:** To examine the importance of being honest with oneself in building family communication.

DISCUSSION QUESTIONS
1. What personal barriers can stand in the way of effective family communication?
2. What might encourage parents to reason with a child even when it is apparent that the child is not open to the parents' opinions? How does the child frequently respond to the parents' efforts?
3. How capable are young people of various ages in making decisions for themselves? What is the parents' role in helping a child make wise choices?
4. How often do we as parents take time to see ourselves through the eyes of our children? How can this communication skill enhance family relationships?

ASSIGNMENTS
1. After you have had a discussion with your child, reflect on your conversation. Write down what you think your child thought while the two of you were talking. Invite your child to read what you have written. Ask for an evaluation of the accuracy of your perceptions.
2. Take an inventory of the messages you were given by your parents about how you should relate to other family members. Now work to identify the negative ways you communicate with your family members. Which of these communication habits

result from your past? Work on discarding those that are not useful to your family.

**BIBLICAL REFERENCE:** Psalm 46
This psalm identifies many forces that create tension within people. This tension can place a barrier between us and God. If we allow ourselves to "be still" and know God, we find that in the process we also discover the unshakable strength that can move us to become all we are capable of being—in spite of what we endured in the past.

### ❖ SESSION TWELVE ❖

**READ:** Chapters 22 and 23.
**OBJECTIVE:** To learn how parental leadership and effective communication work together to give direction to the family.

DISCUSSION QUESTIONS
1. In what ways do parents struggle to gain control over a child? How can efforts to control a child cause the parent-child relationship to deteriorate?
2. What are the ways adults and children attempt to control one another? How do the methods of parents differ from the tactics of children?
3. How does family communication contribute to the way family members cooperate with one another?
4. What makes it difficult for adults to view matters from a child's point of view?

ASSIGNMENTS
1. Play a game with your child. Let him or her make all the rules. Even if your child is not playing the game the right way, refrain from making any corrections or negative comments. The important point is that you allow your child to feel capable of making decisions.
2. After you have had an argument with your child, on your own, sit back and recreate the conversation you and your child had. Determine as honestly as you can how closely your spoken words and nonverbal messages matched up.

**BIBLICAL REFERENCE:** Psalm 19:1-4,14

In this psalm, David acknowledges that God's creation is a statement of His greatness. There can be no uncertainty of the accuracy of God's communication to us because His word is forever true. David concludes this psalm by humbly expressing hope that his words would always be seen as a true statement of his inner feelings. David's desire for harmony in his words and outward expressions can be ours as well.

## ❖ SESSION THIRTEEN ❖

**READ:** Chapters 24 and 25.

**OBJECTIVE:** To learn of the healing strength of relationships among family members.

### DISCUSSION QUESTIONS

1. How can parents identify too strongly with the feelings of a child? In what ways can this over-identification be harmful?
2. What ways does a child send the message to parents that he wants greater freedom?
3. What healing powers are found when relationships among family members are marked by closeness? How would you define a healthy relationship between a parent and a child?
4. What might parents do that keeps a child from wanting a close parent-child relationship? What can the adults do to promote closeness in the family?
5. How do we put conditions on our love for our children?

### ASSIGNMENTS

1. Make a concerted effort to find activities you and your child can enjoy together. Take time regularly to engage in these activities.
2. Each day for the next week give your child a hug or some other gesture of affection when you come home at the end of the day (or when your child comes home). Note the reaction your child has to your gesture.

**BIBLICAL REFERENCE:** 2 Timothy 1:2-7
In this poignant passage, we see the affection that Paul shared with young Timothy, whom he considered as a son. We can be sure that the strength of this relationship was a teaching tool that allowed Paul to have a great influence over Timothy.

# Notes

CHAPTER 2: *Why Can't I Control My Emotions?*
1. 1 Thessalonians 5:14-15.

CHAPTER 3: *Why Do I Feel So Isolated and Alone?*
1. John 4:7-30.

CHAPTER 5: *Why Am I Sad When I Want to Be Happy?*
1. Psalm 138:7-8.

CHAPTER 7: *Why Do I Feel So Lousy About Me?*
1. Psalm 139:23-34.

CHAPTER 8: *Understanding Why I Can't Stand Conflict*
1. Proverbs 1:8-9.

CHAPTER 10: *Understanding Why I Fear Negative Feelings*
1. Romans 12:2.

CHAPTER 11: *Understanding Why I Overpower My Child*
1. Zechariah 4:6.

CHAPTER 12: *Understanding Why I Can't Face Reality*
1. Matthew 6:12,14.
2. Mark 3:1-5, John 8:3-7.

CHAPTER 13: *Exchanging Mistrust for Trust*
1. Psalm 8.
2. Psalm 37:3,5.

CHAPTER 14: *Exchanging Unhappiness for Satisfaction*
1. Matthew 10:8.

CHAPTER 15: *Exchanging Frustration for Gratitude*
1. Romans 7:15.
2. Romans 7:21-25.
3. 2 Timothy 1:13.

CHAPTER 16: *Exchanging Withdrawal for Relationship*
1. Luke 12:32.

CHAPTER 18: *Exchanging Control for Boundaries*
1. Galatians 5:22-23.

CHAPTER 19: *Exchanging Conflict for Choices/Consequences*
1. Mark 2:1-12.

PART 4: *Leaving the Past Behind*
1. Matthew 5:48.
2. Leviticus 19:2.

CHAPTER 20: *Listening*
1. Psalm 139:1-4.
2. Psalm 139:23-24.

CHAPTER 21: *Examining*
1. Matthew 7:3-5.

CHAPTER 22: *Influencing*
1. Ephesians 6:4.
2. Romans 8:38-39.

CHAPTER 23: *Warming*
1. Matthew 19:14.

CHAPTER 24: *Separating*
1. Philippians 4:5-9.

CHAPTER 25: *Relating*
1. Psalm 139:23-24.

*Epilogue*
1. 2 Corinthians 13:11.

# *Author*

Wm. Lee Carter, Ed.D., is a psychologist at Child Psychiatry Associates, a group private practice in Waco, Texas. He is a licensed psychologist, having earned his doctoral degree from Baylor University. In his practice, Dr. Carter counsels children, adolescents, and their families. He is on staff at several Central Texas inpatient and residential treatment facilities.

Previous books include *The Parent-Child Connection* and *Kidthink*. He speaks to varied groups and organizations around the country and is a frequent guest on radio and television shows.

Dr. Clark's greatest learning experiences about children come from his own family interactions. He and his wife, Julie, are parents to three daughters, Emily, Sarah, and Mary.